HOW TO DRAW CUTE ANIMALS

LEARN EASY STEP-BY-STEP TO DRAW KAWAII PETS, A FUN AND SIMPLE STEP BY STEP DRAWING FOR ARTISTS, CARTOONISTS, AND DOODLERS

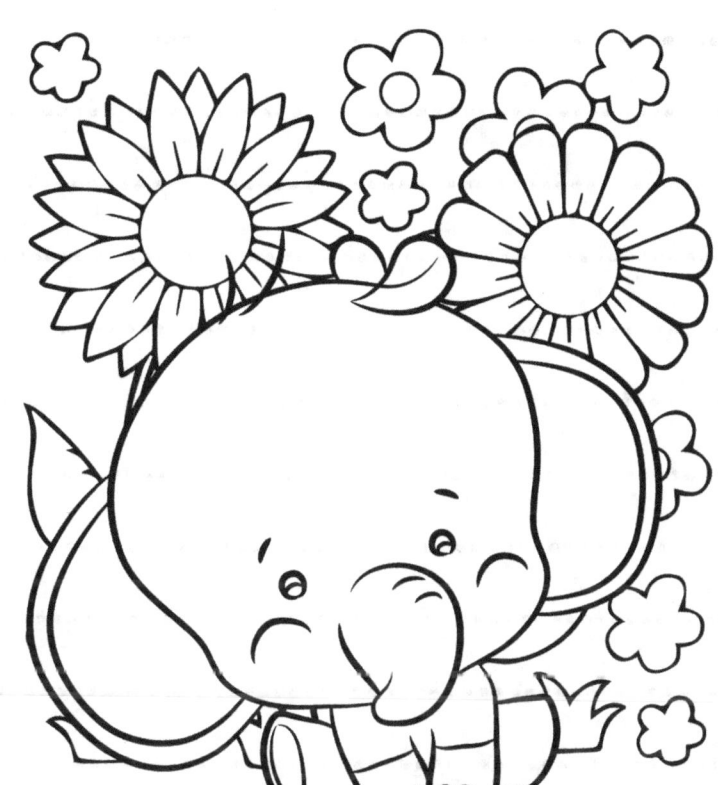

COPYRIGHT © 2019 BY PHOO PUNYA.

BOOK AND COVER DESIGN BY PHOO PUNYA

ISBN: 9781070861265

FIRST EDITION: MAY 2019

TABLE OF CONTENT

HOW TO DRAW CUTE PETS AND ANIMALS

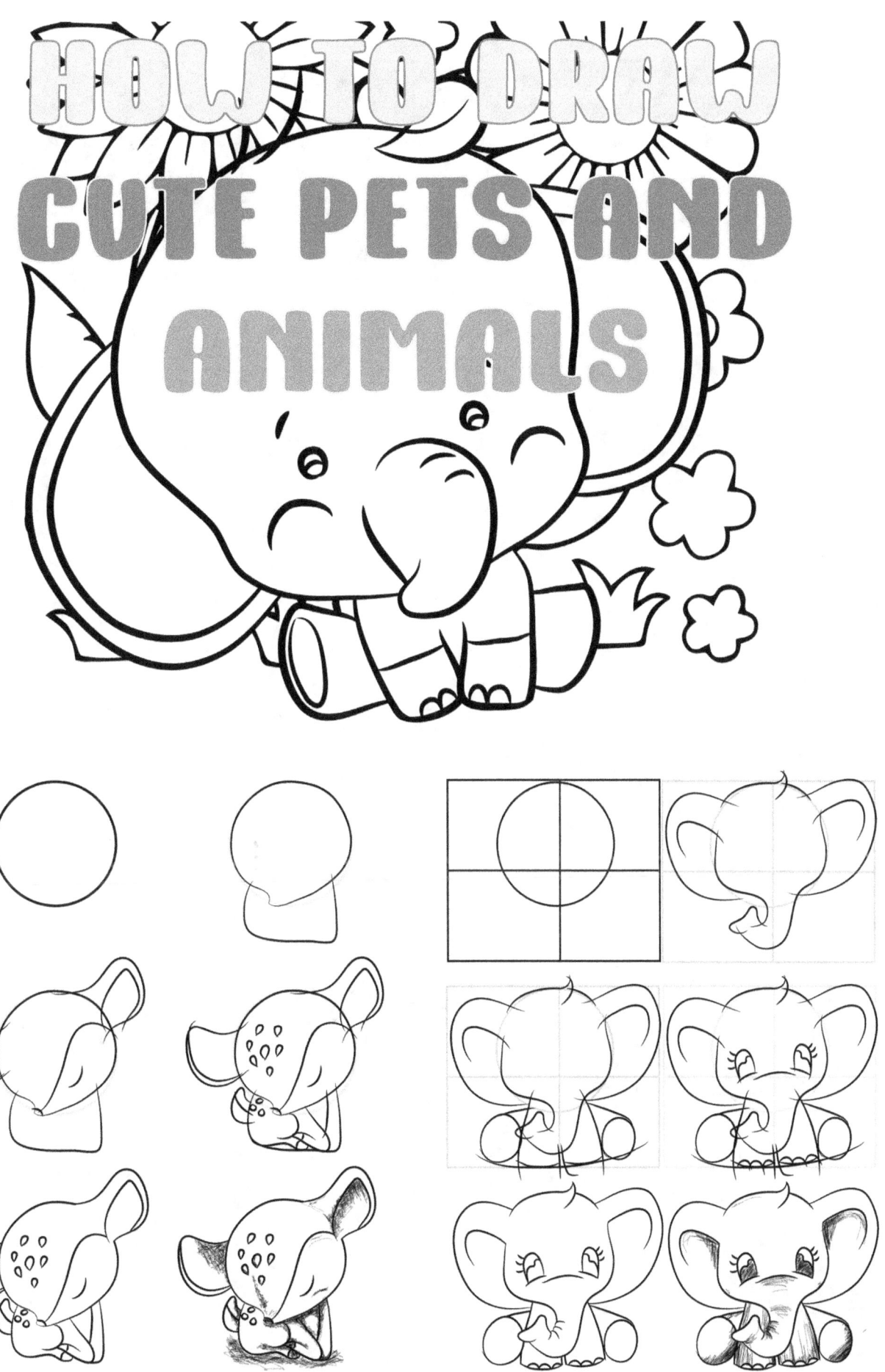

ELEPHANT

SIT

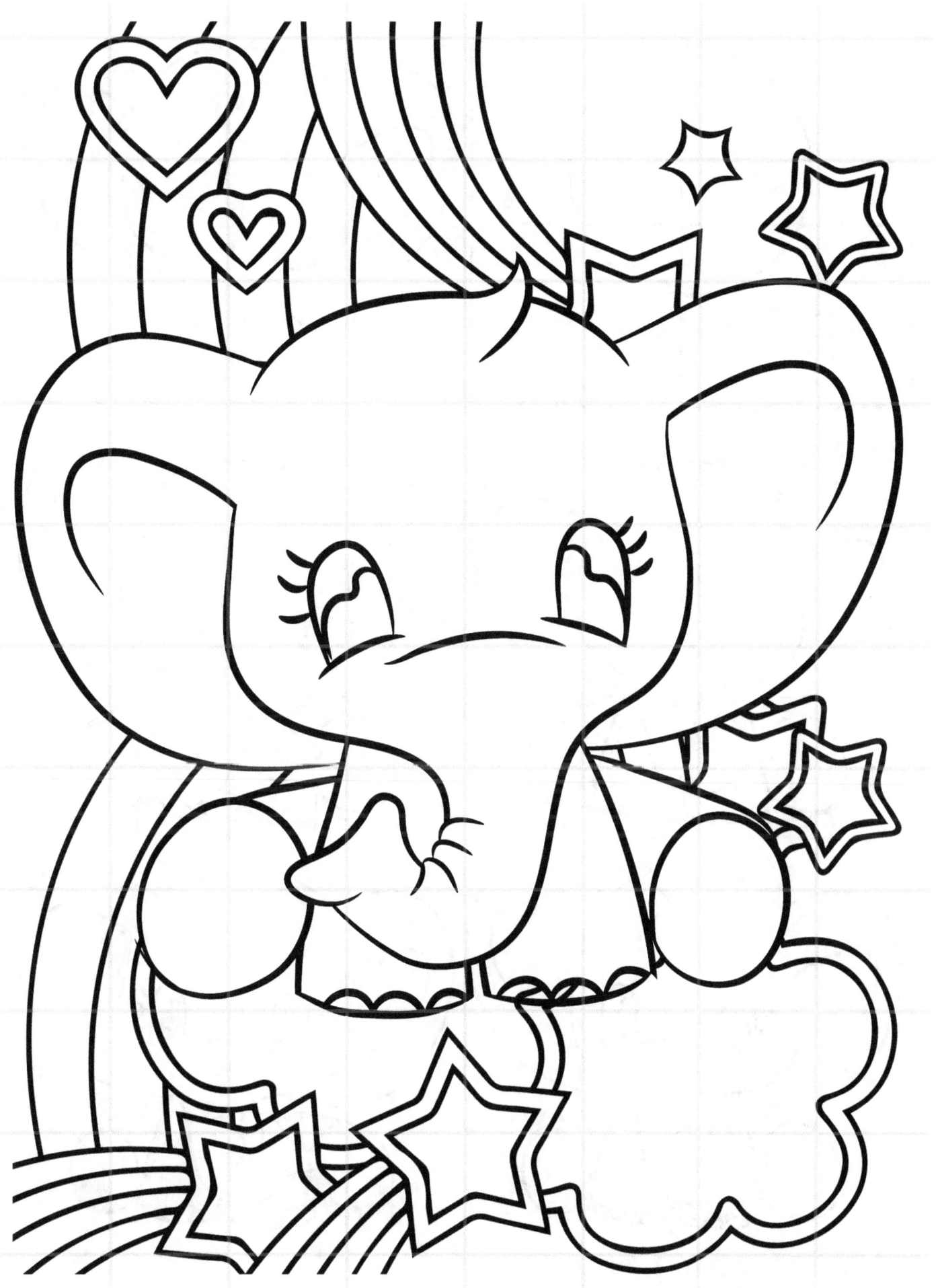

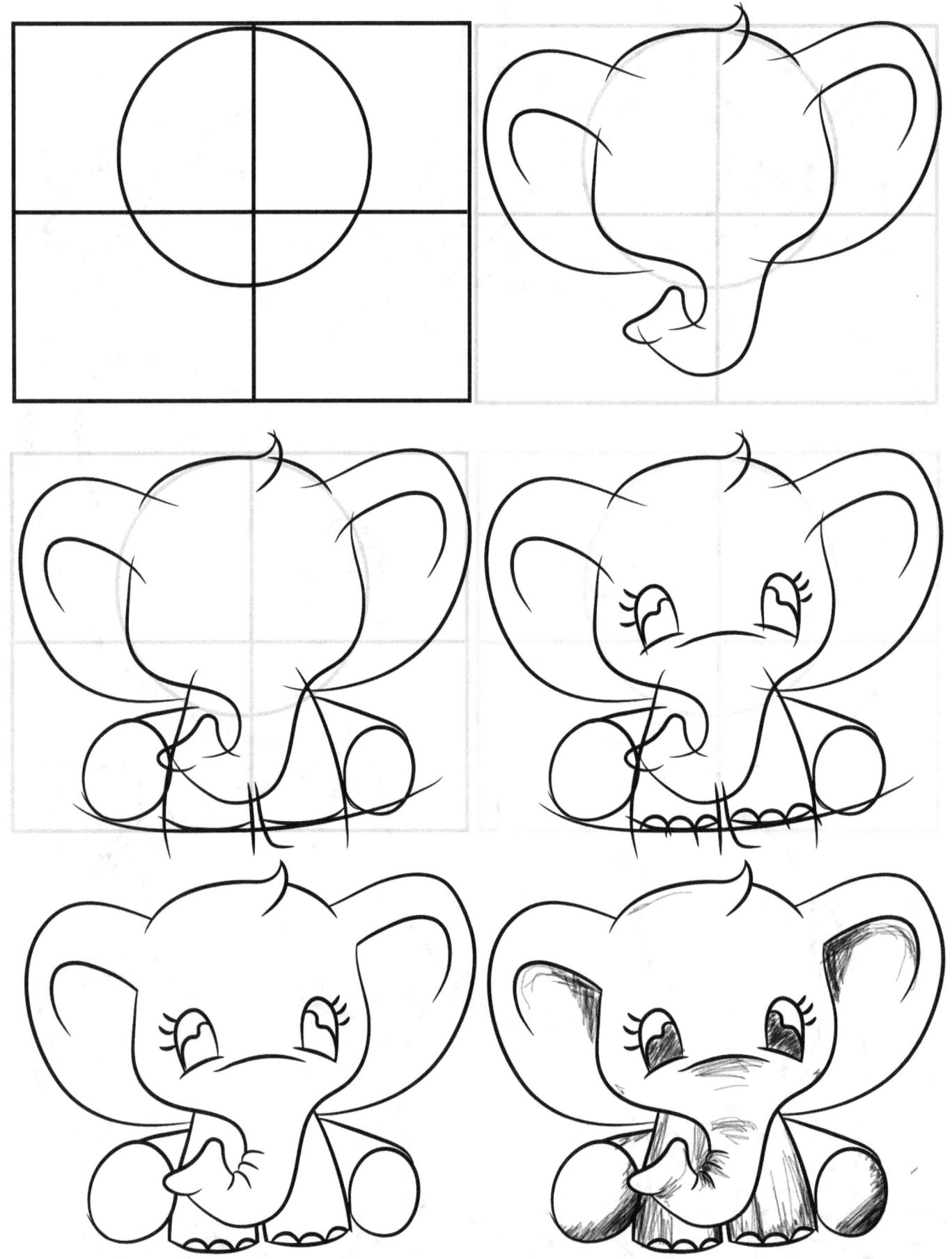

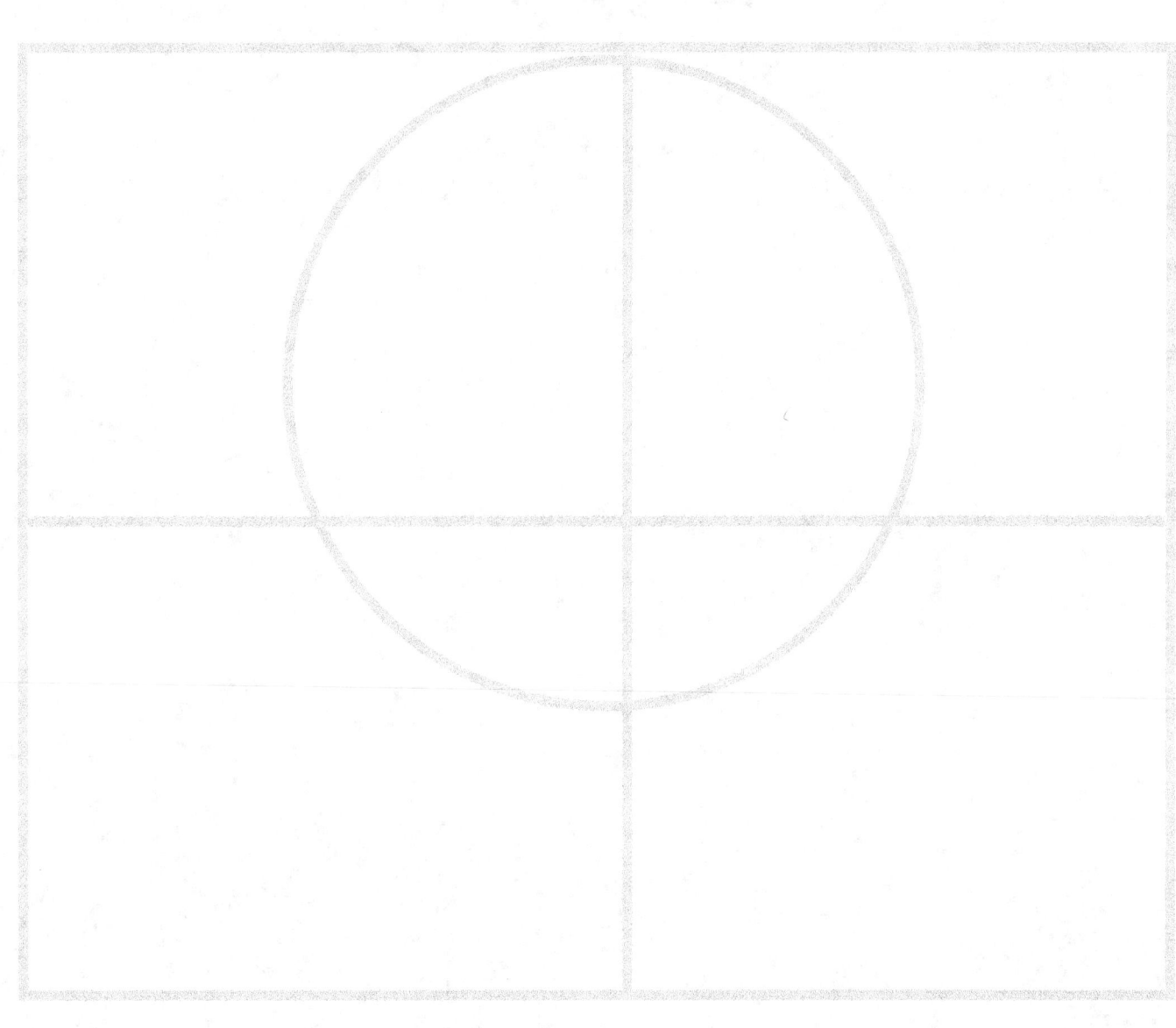

ELEPHANT WALK

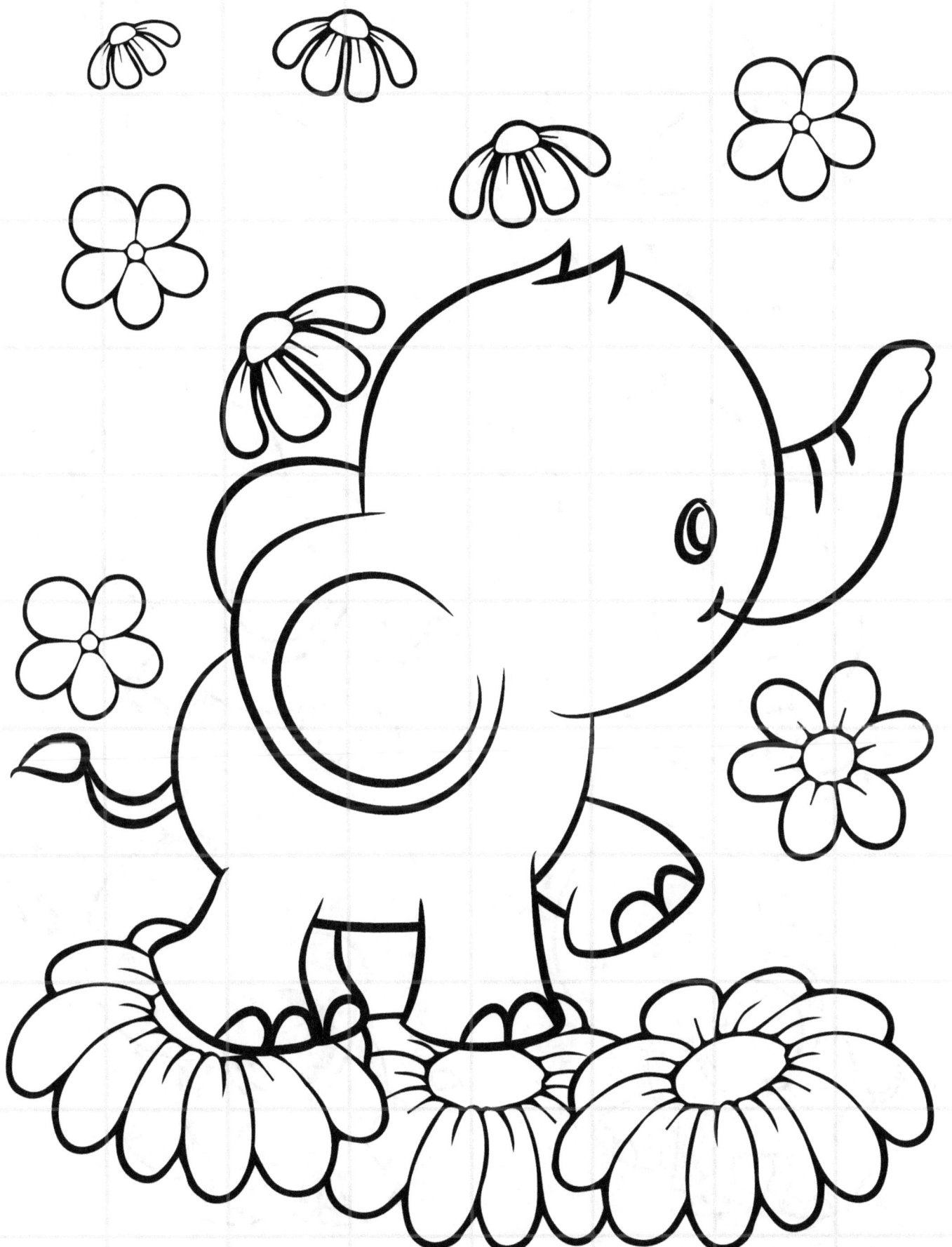

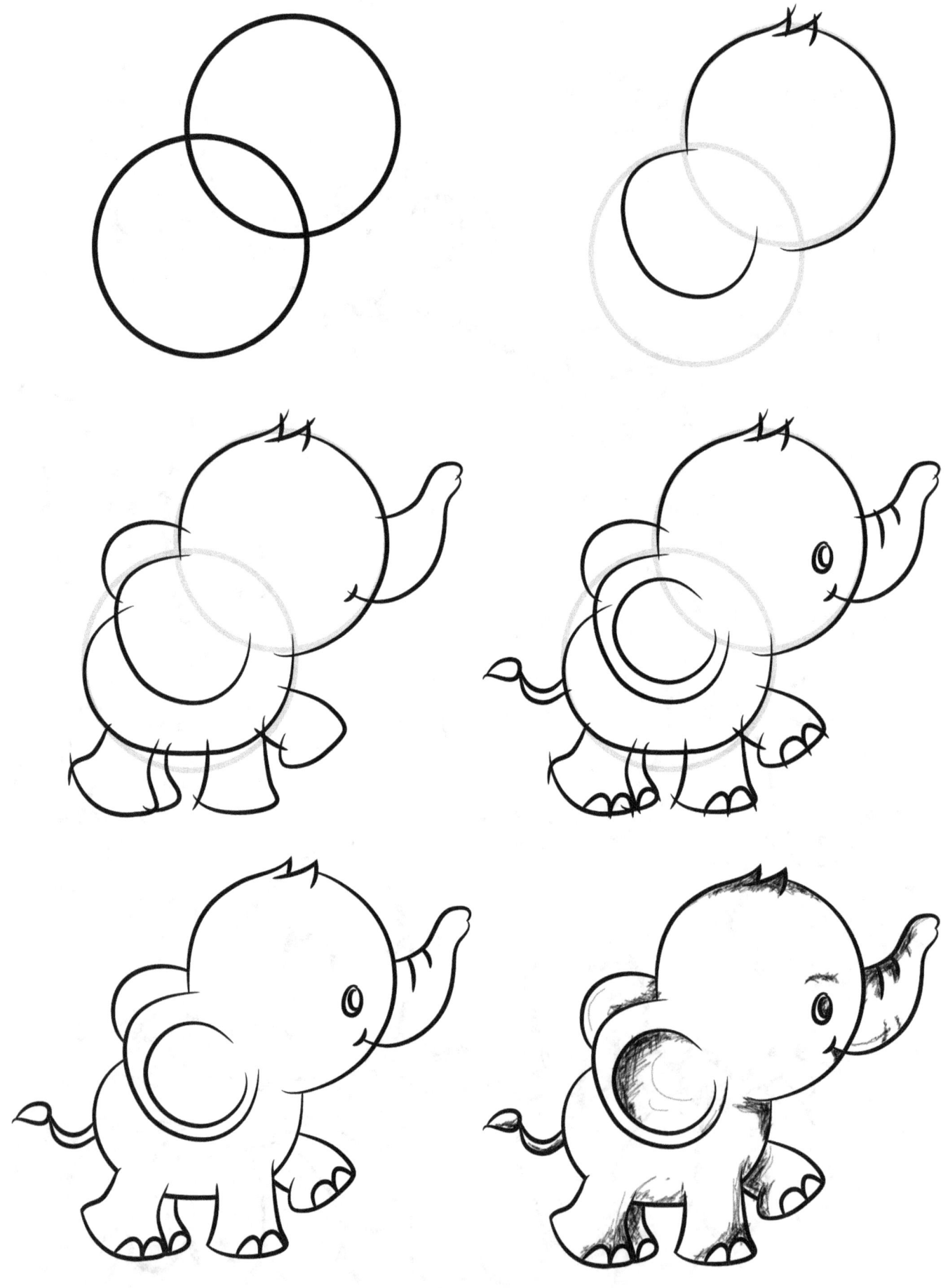

ELEPHANT

SIT

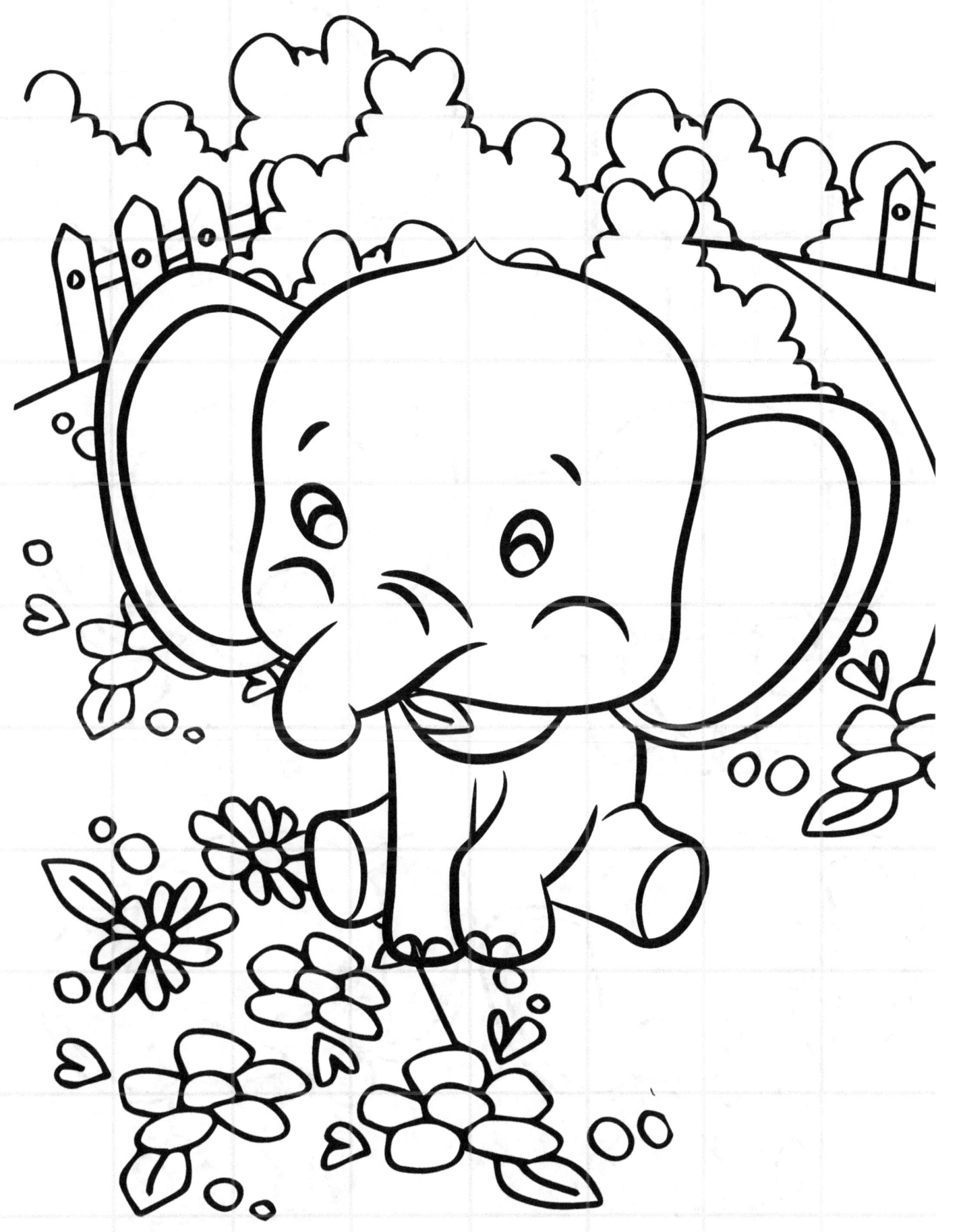

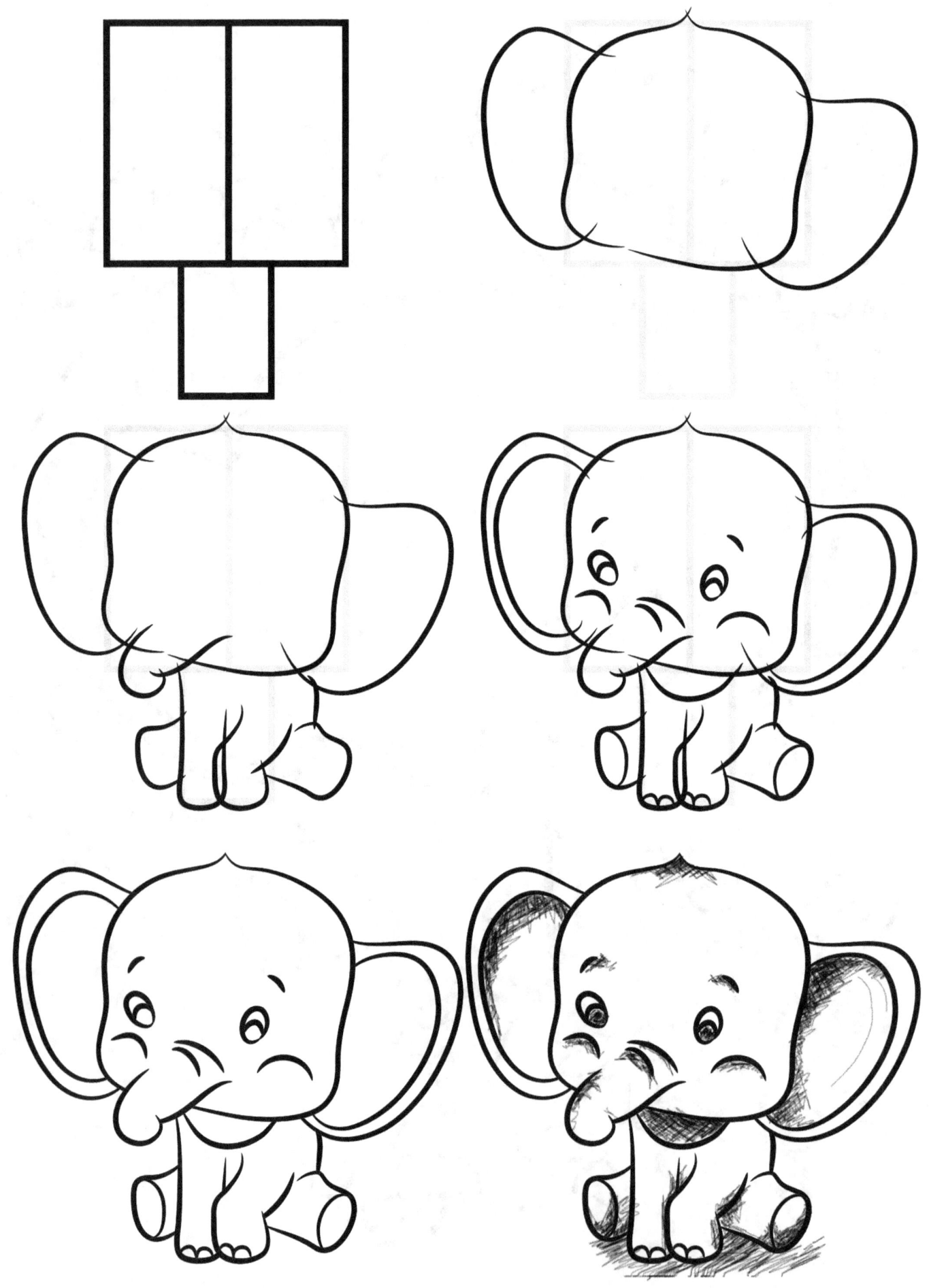

ELEPHANT

SIT

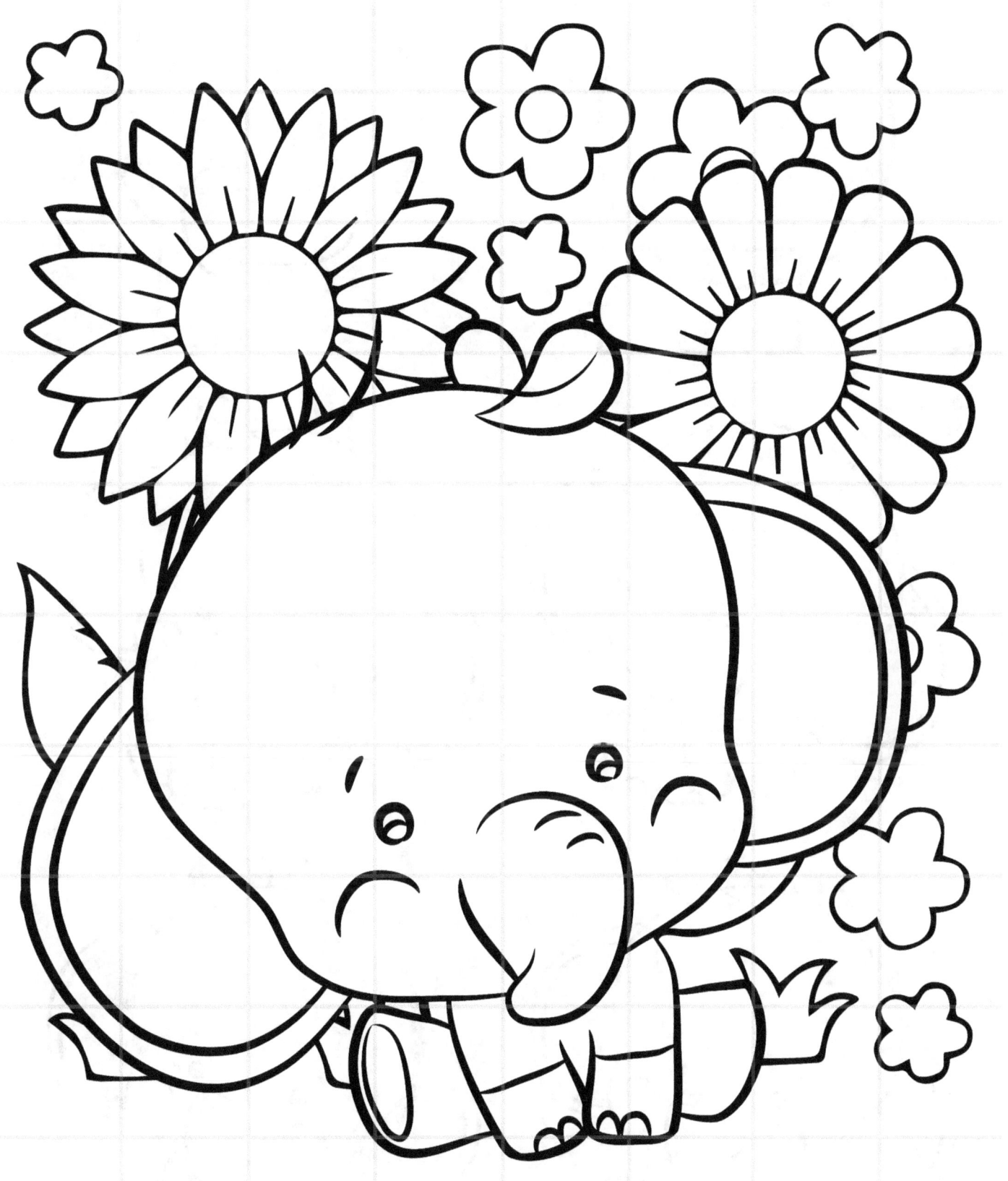

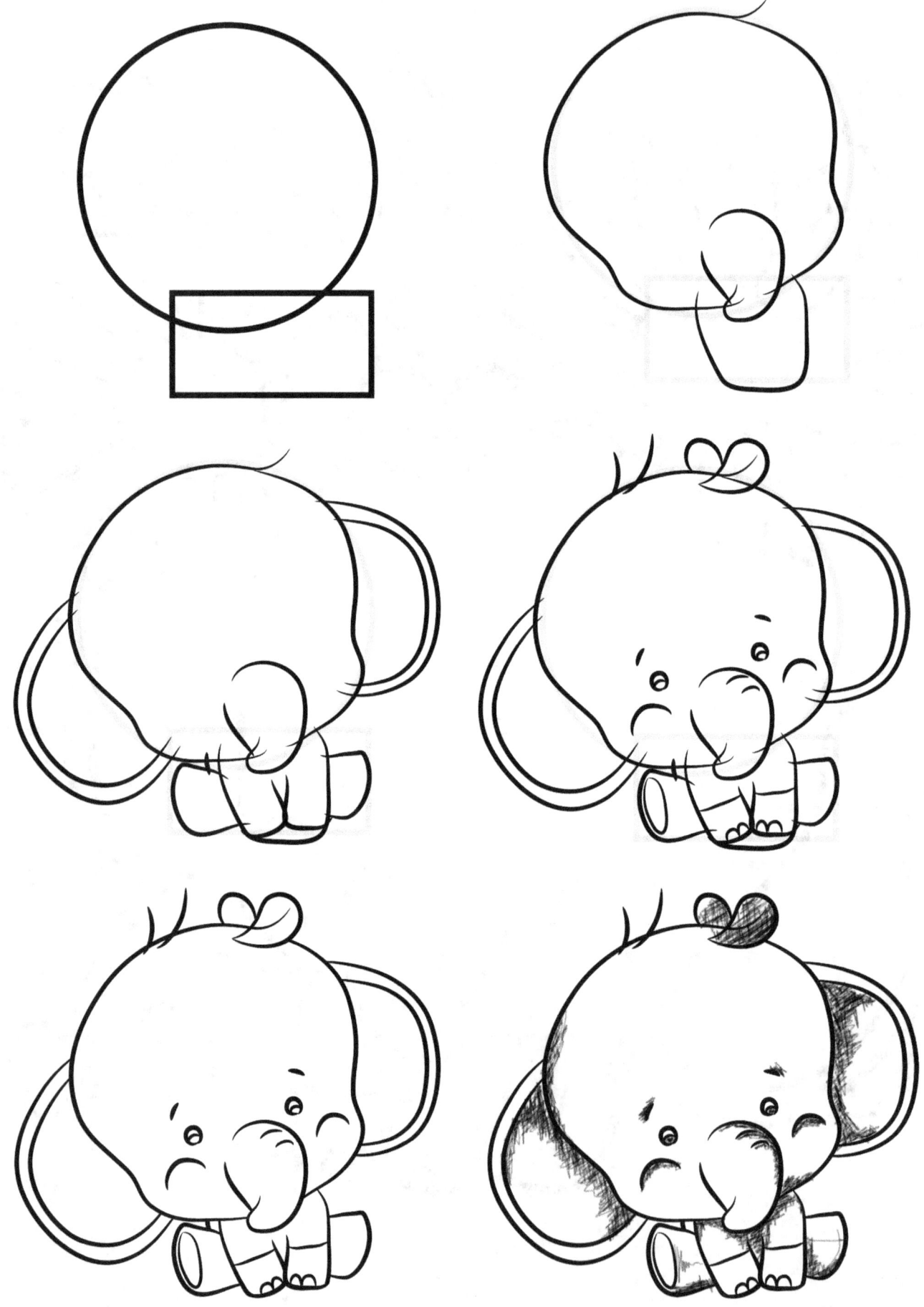

ELEPHANT STAND

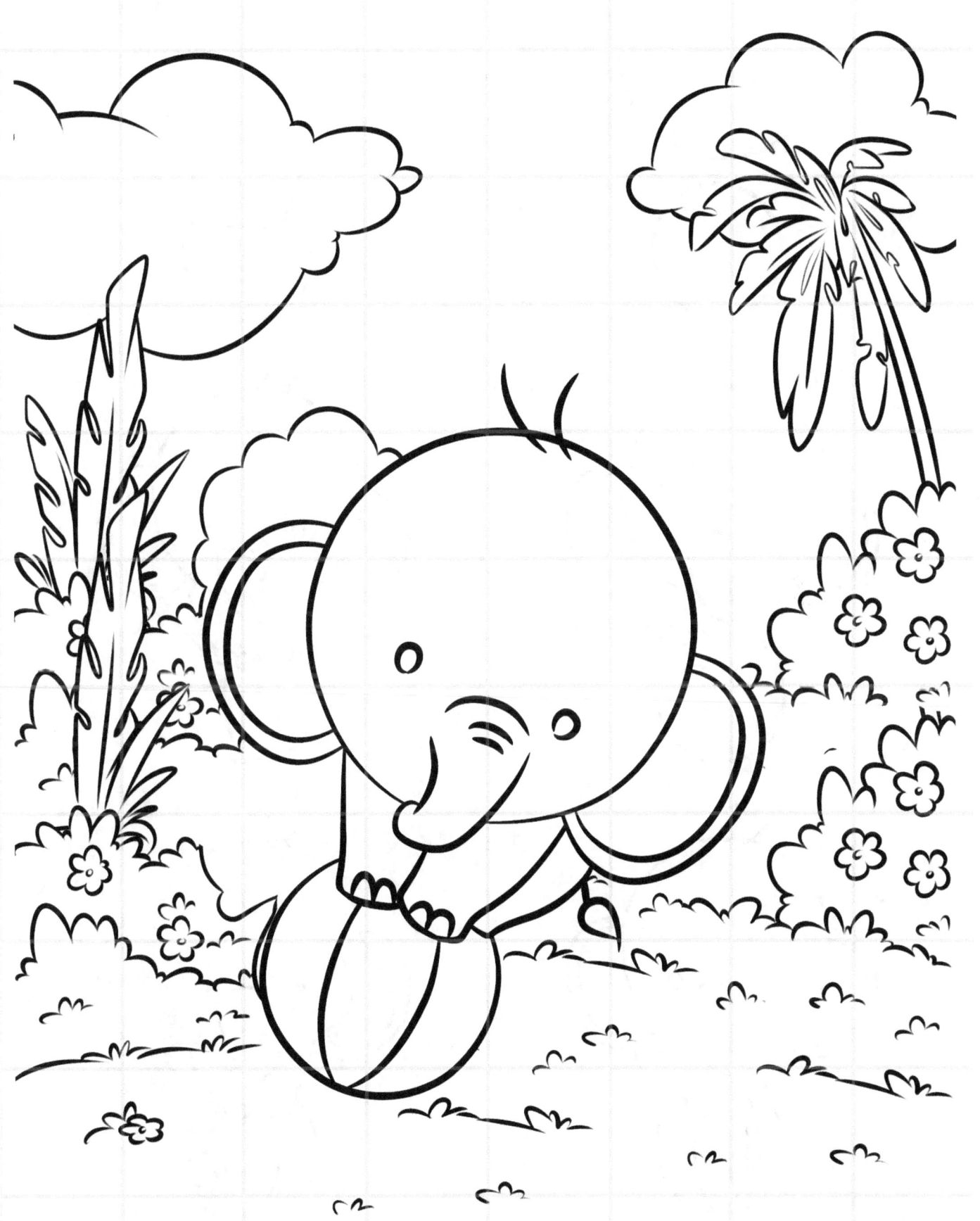

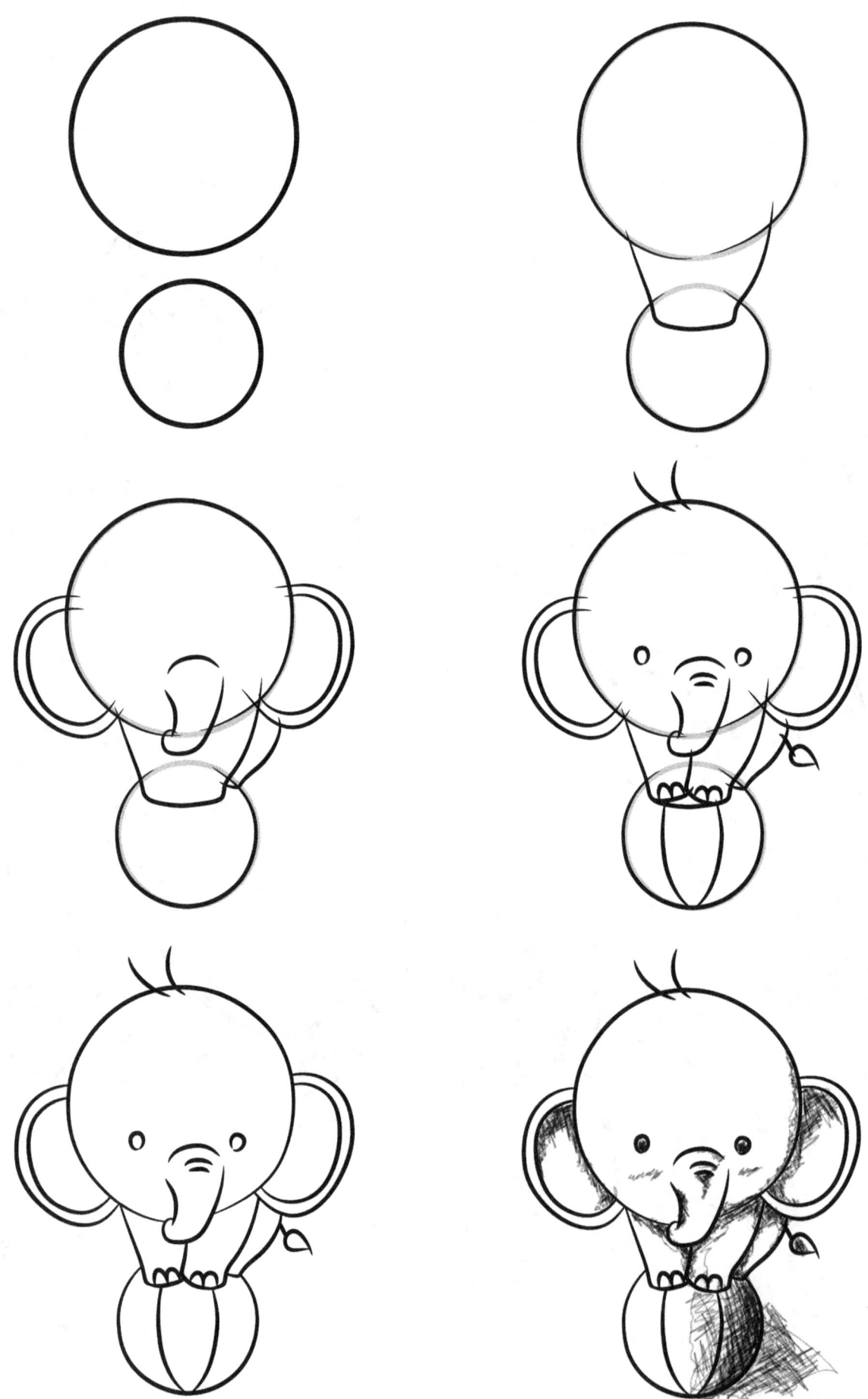

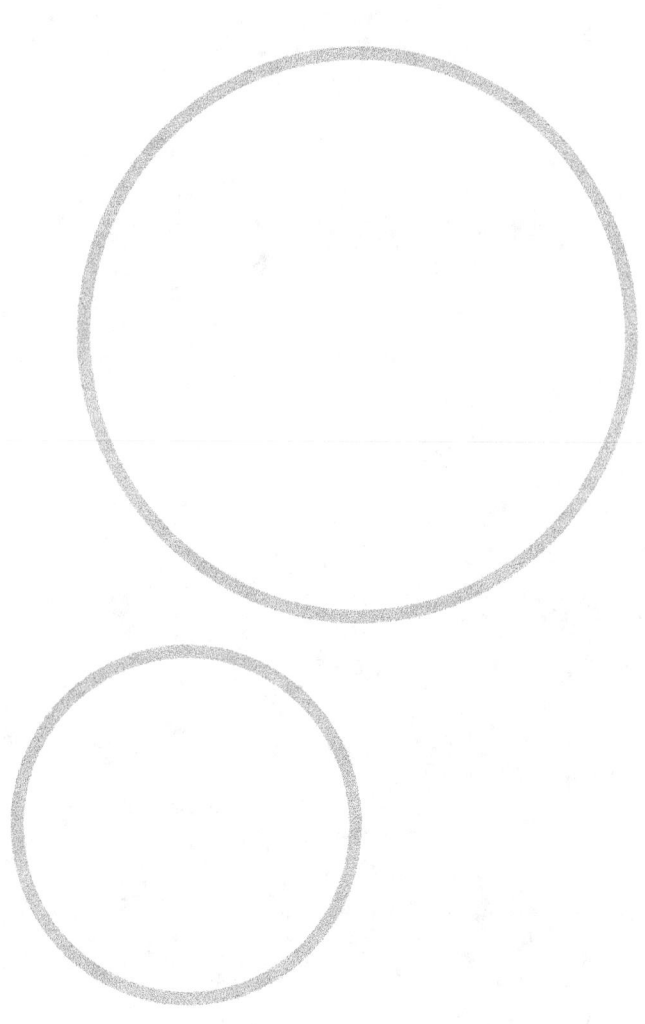

DEER

SIT

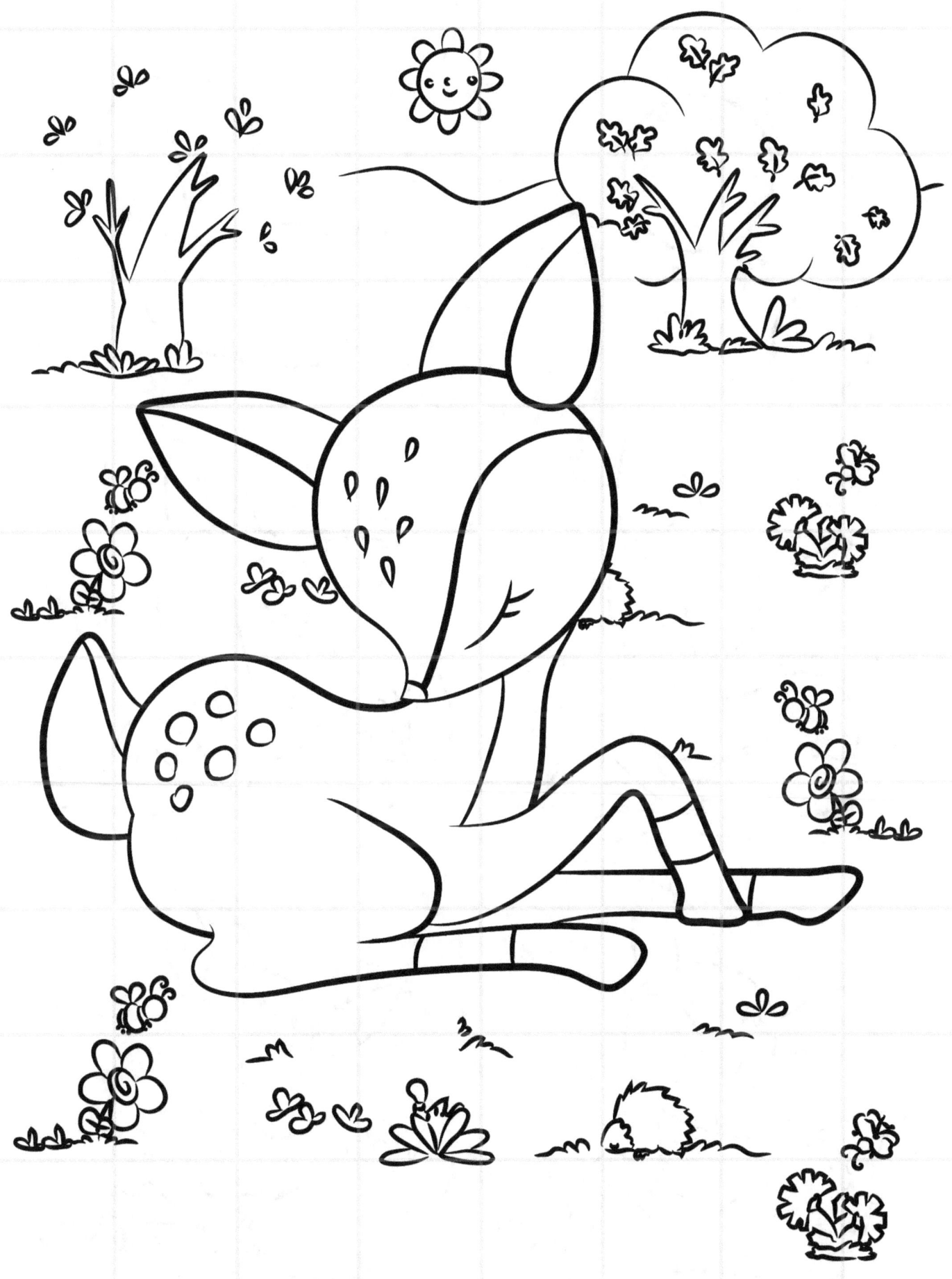

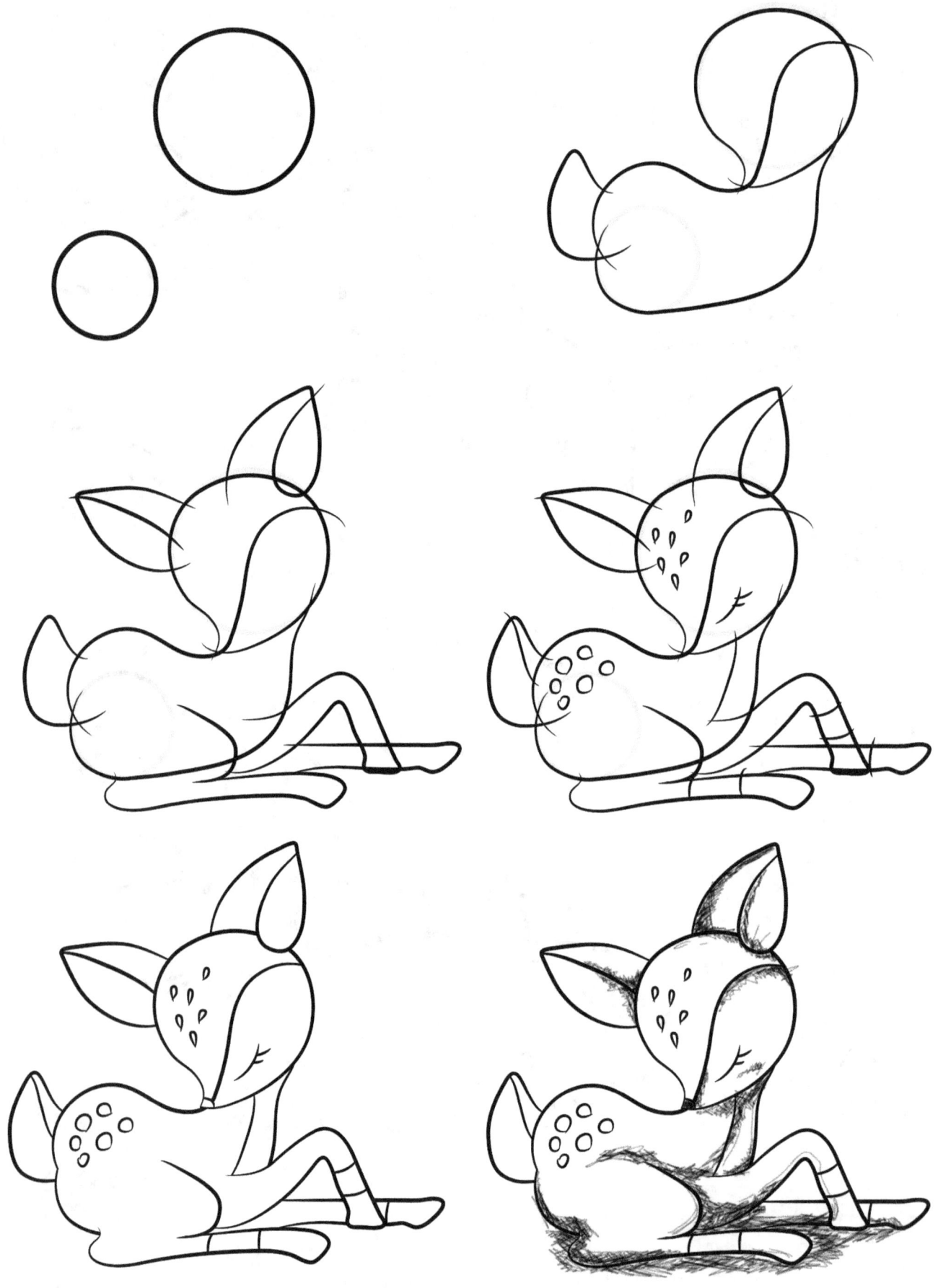

DEER

SLEEP

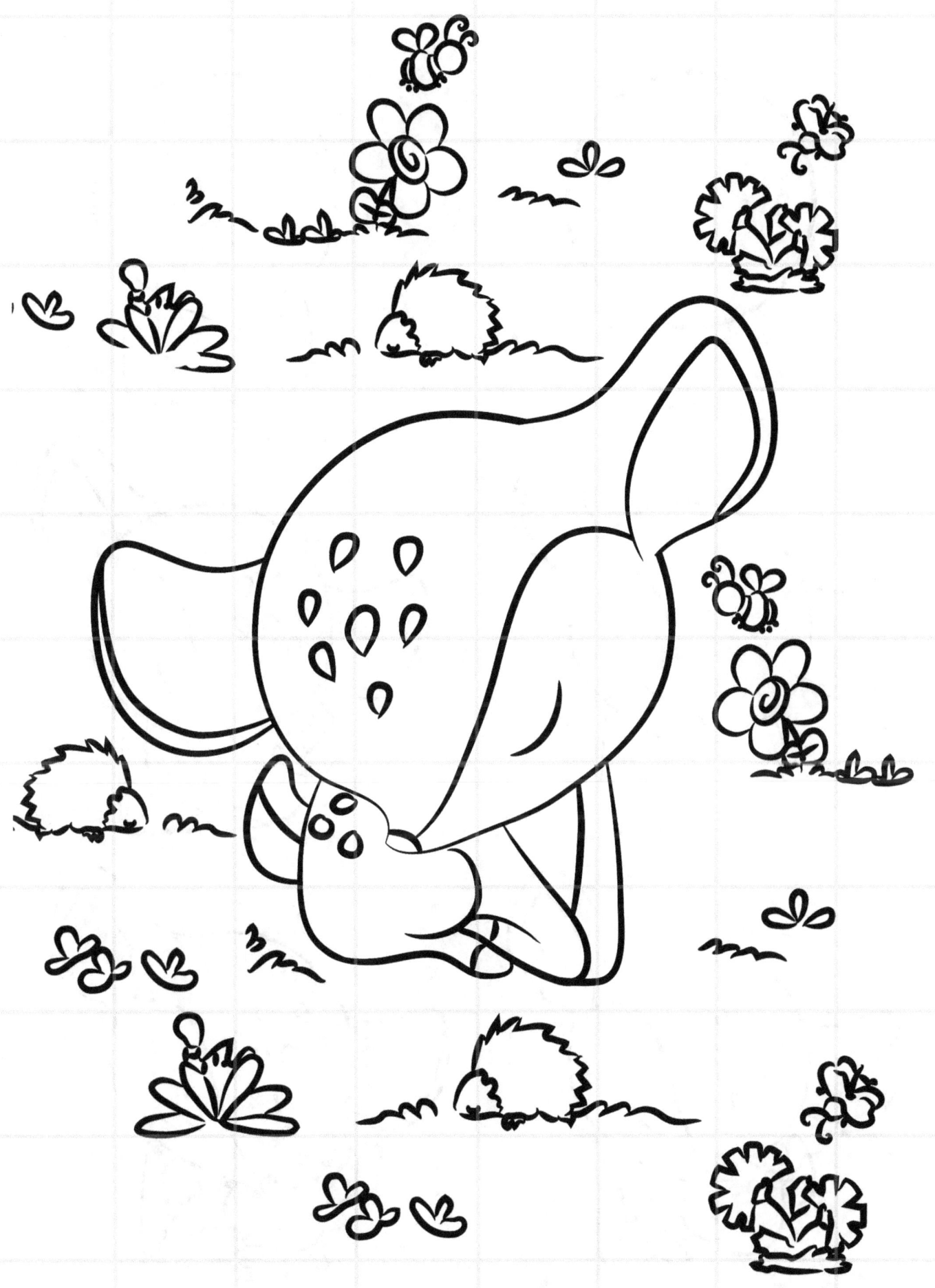

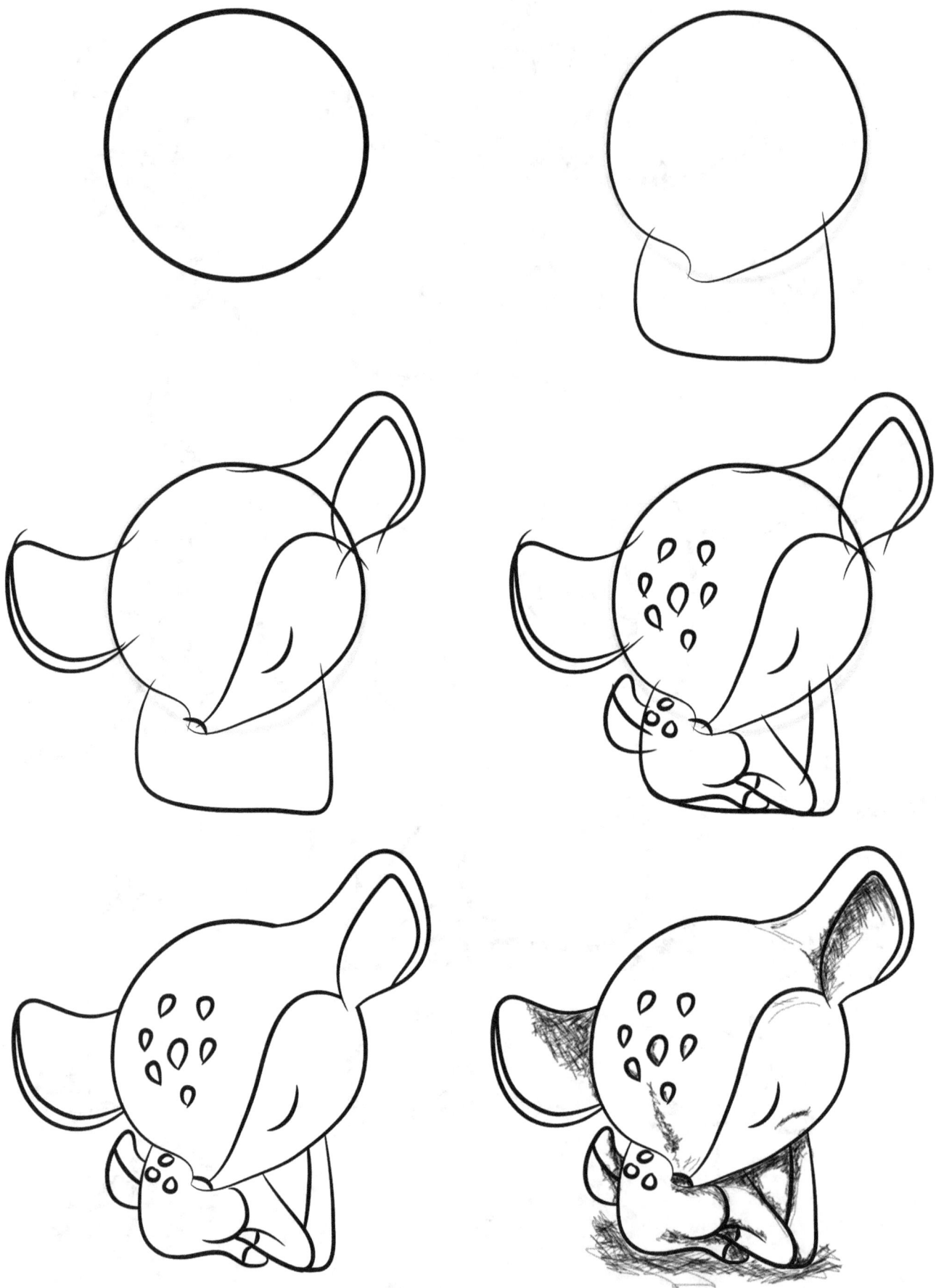

GIRAFFE

SIT

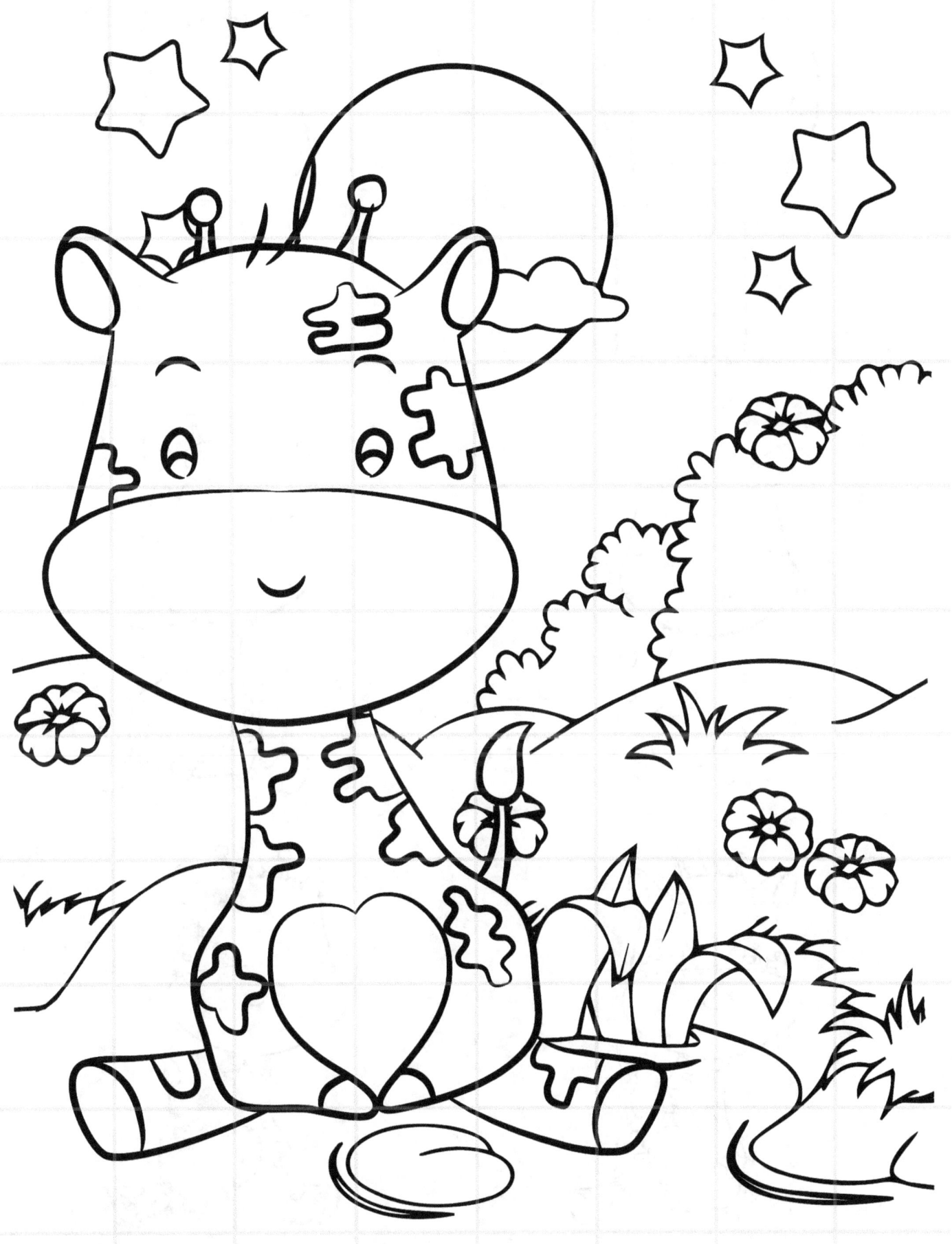

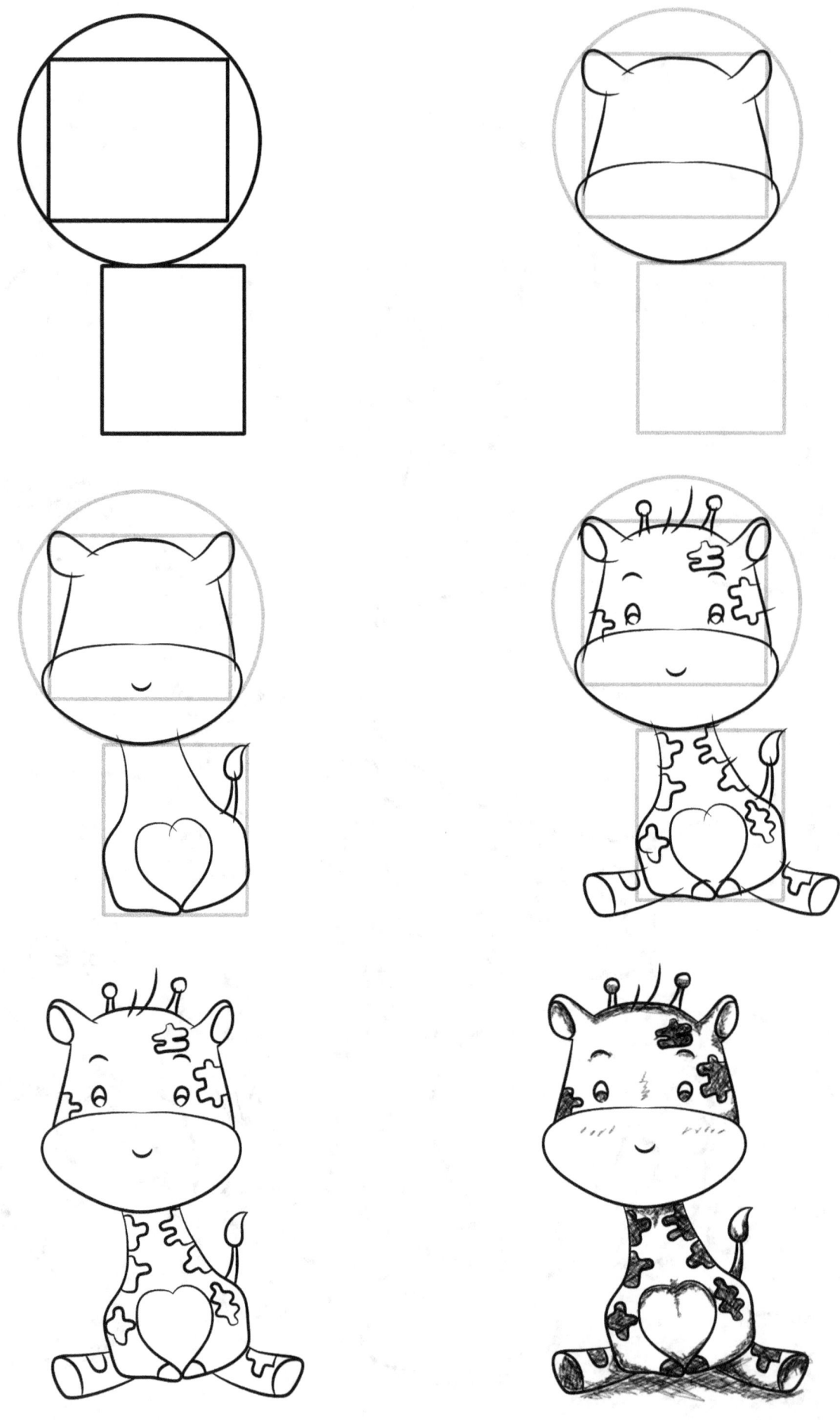

BEAR

STAND

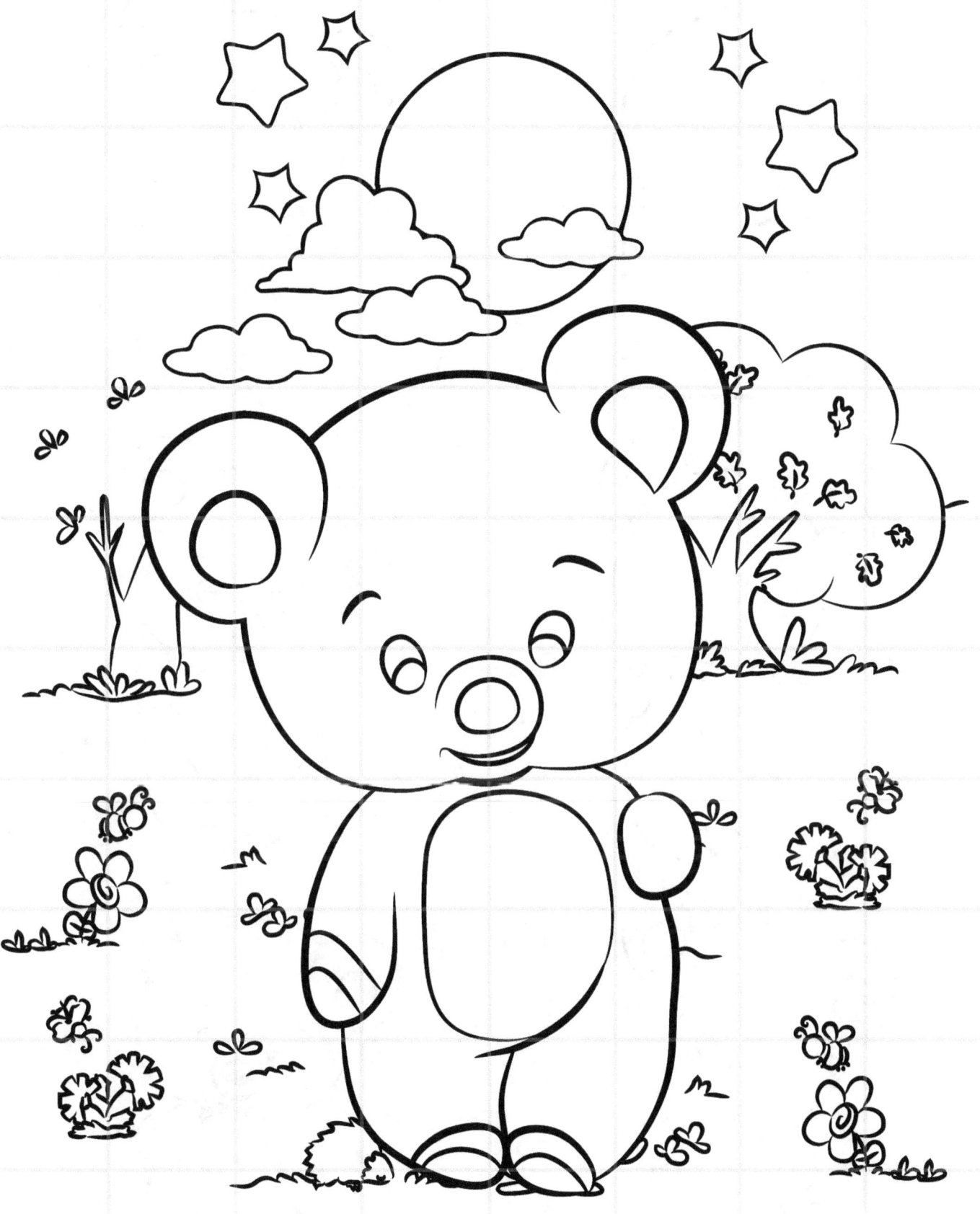

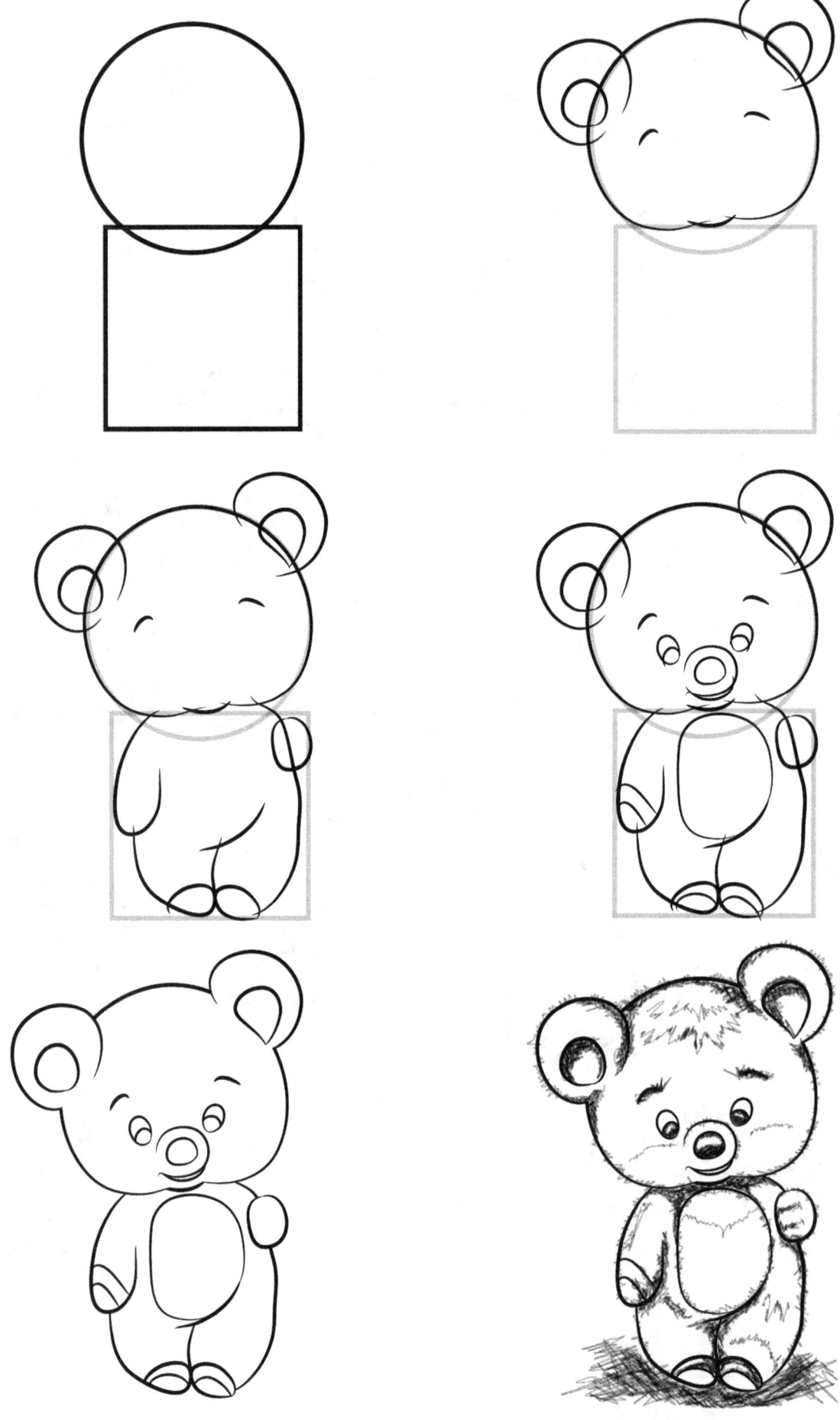

THE LION

SIT

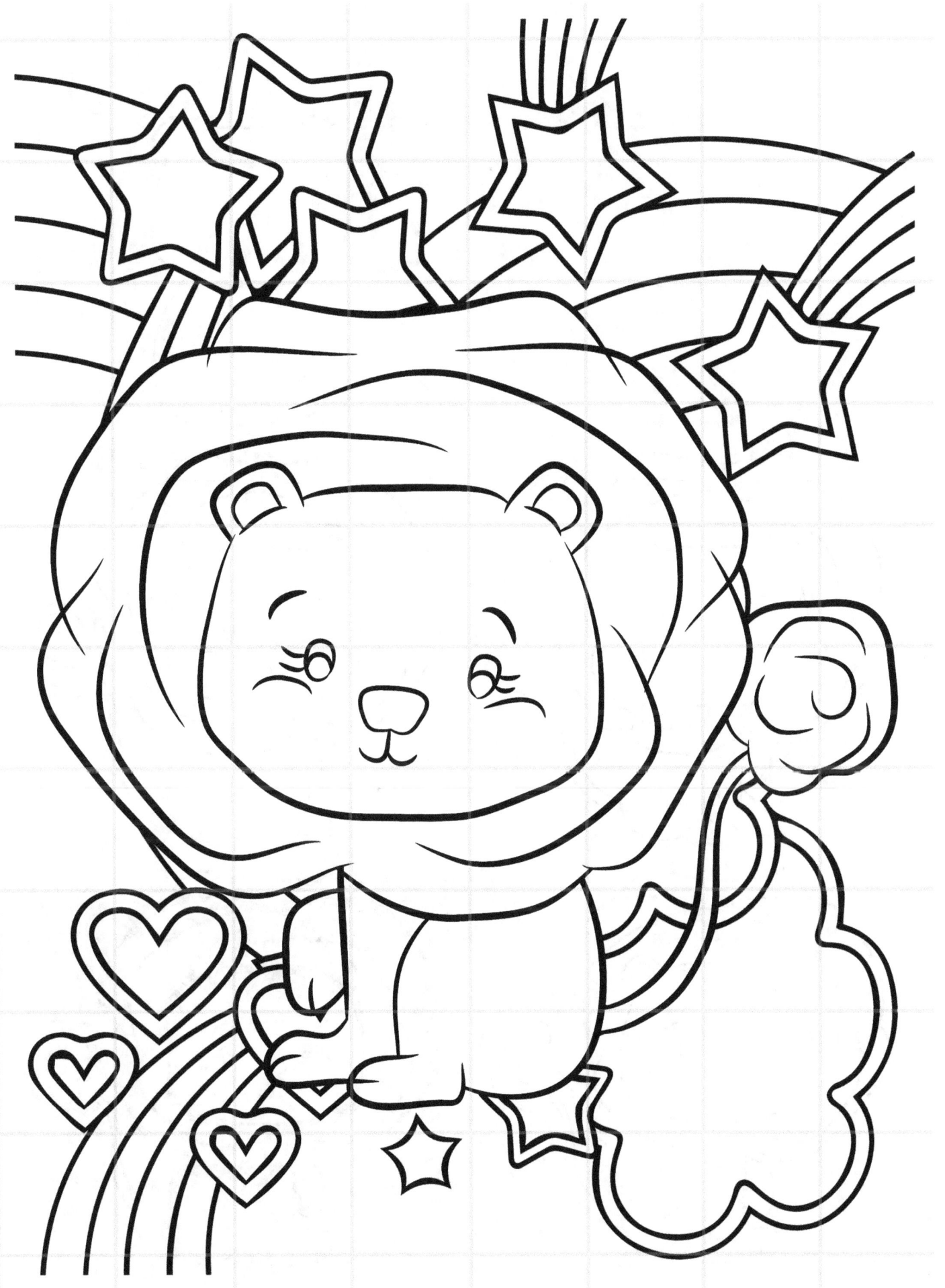

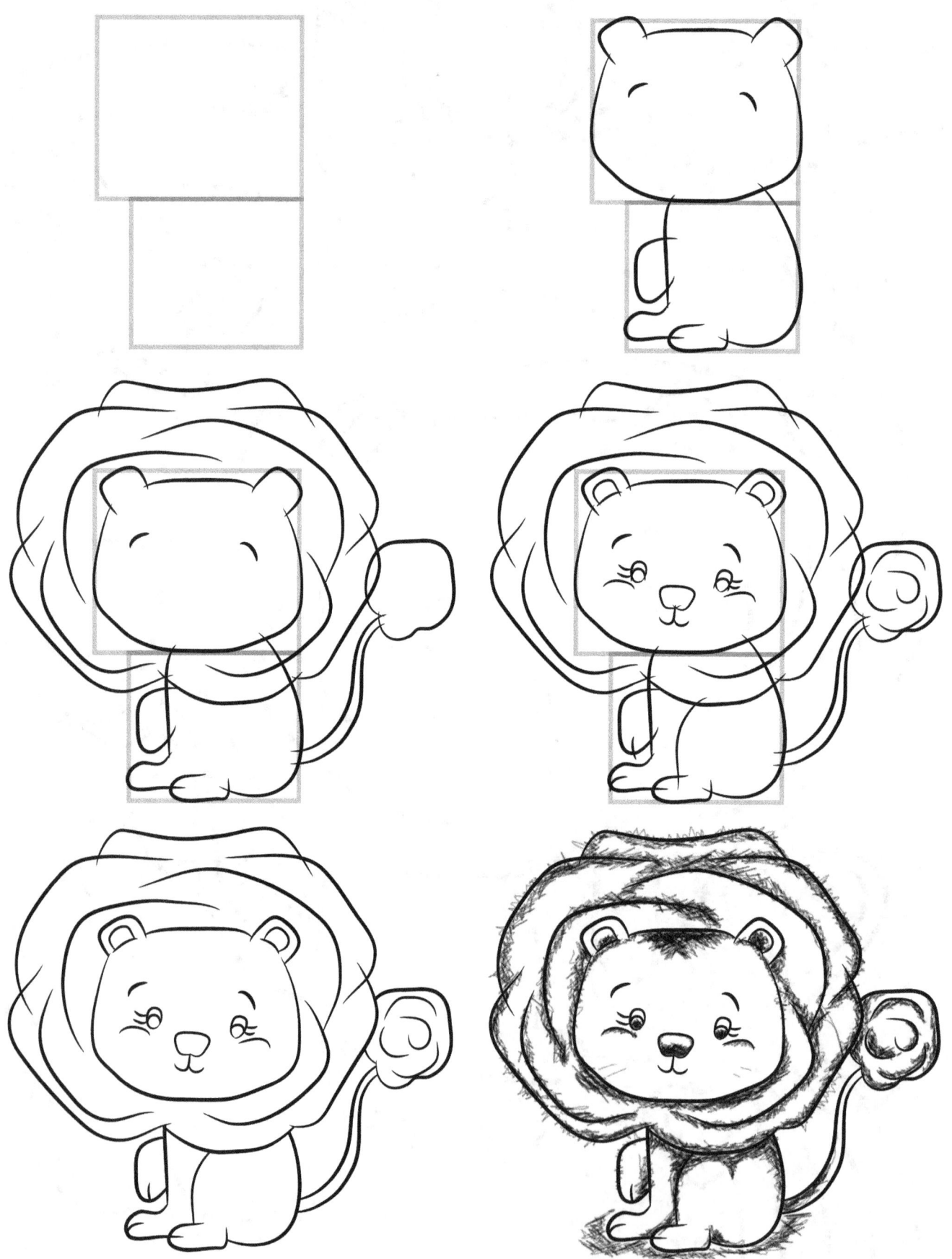

COW

SIT

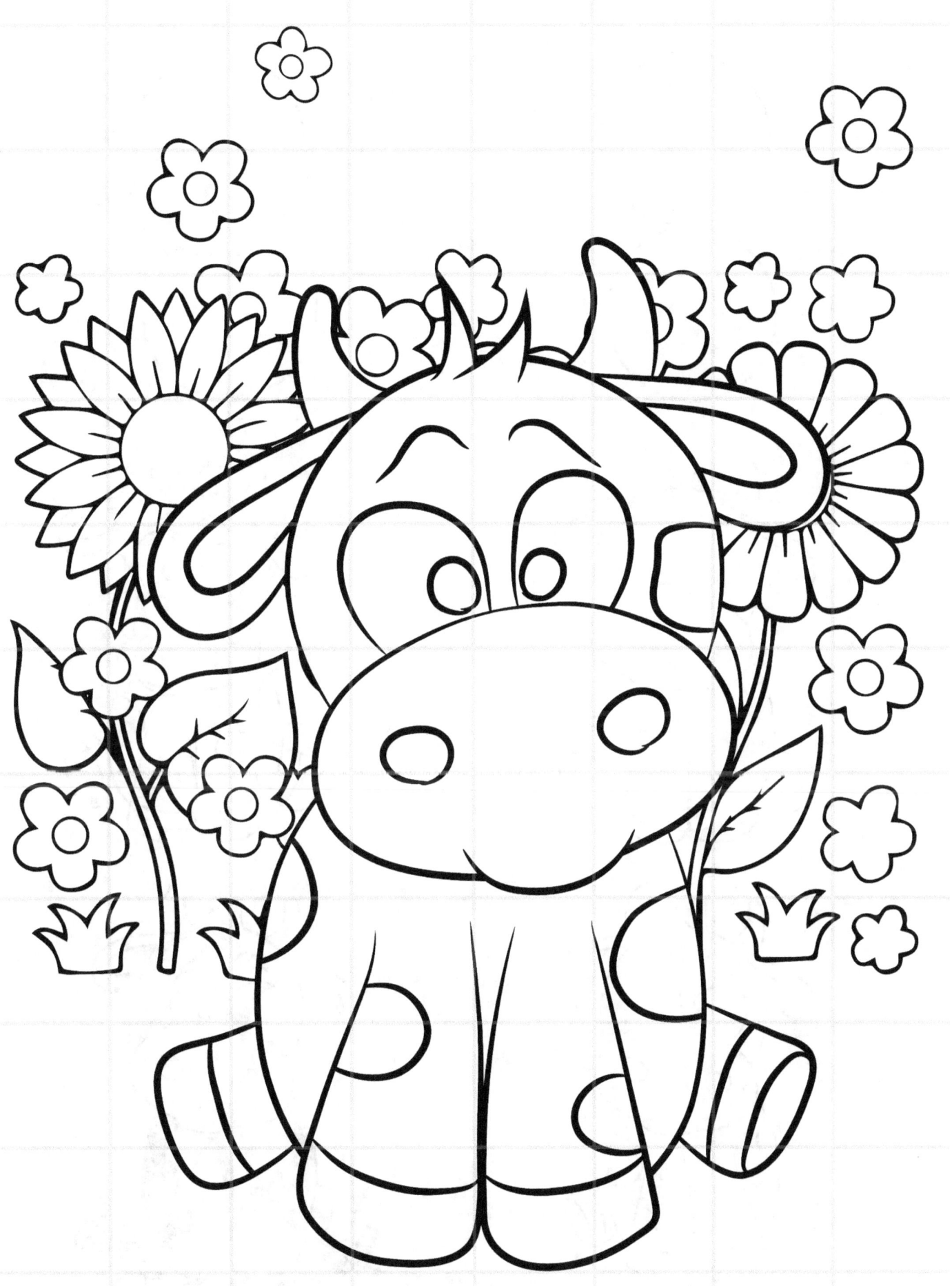

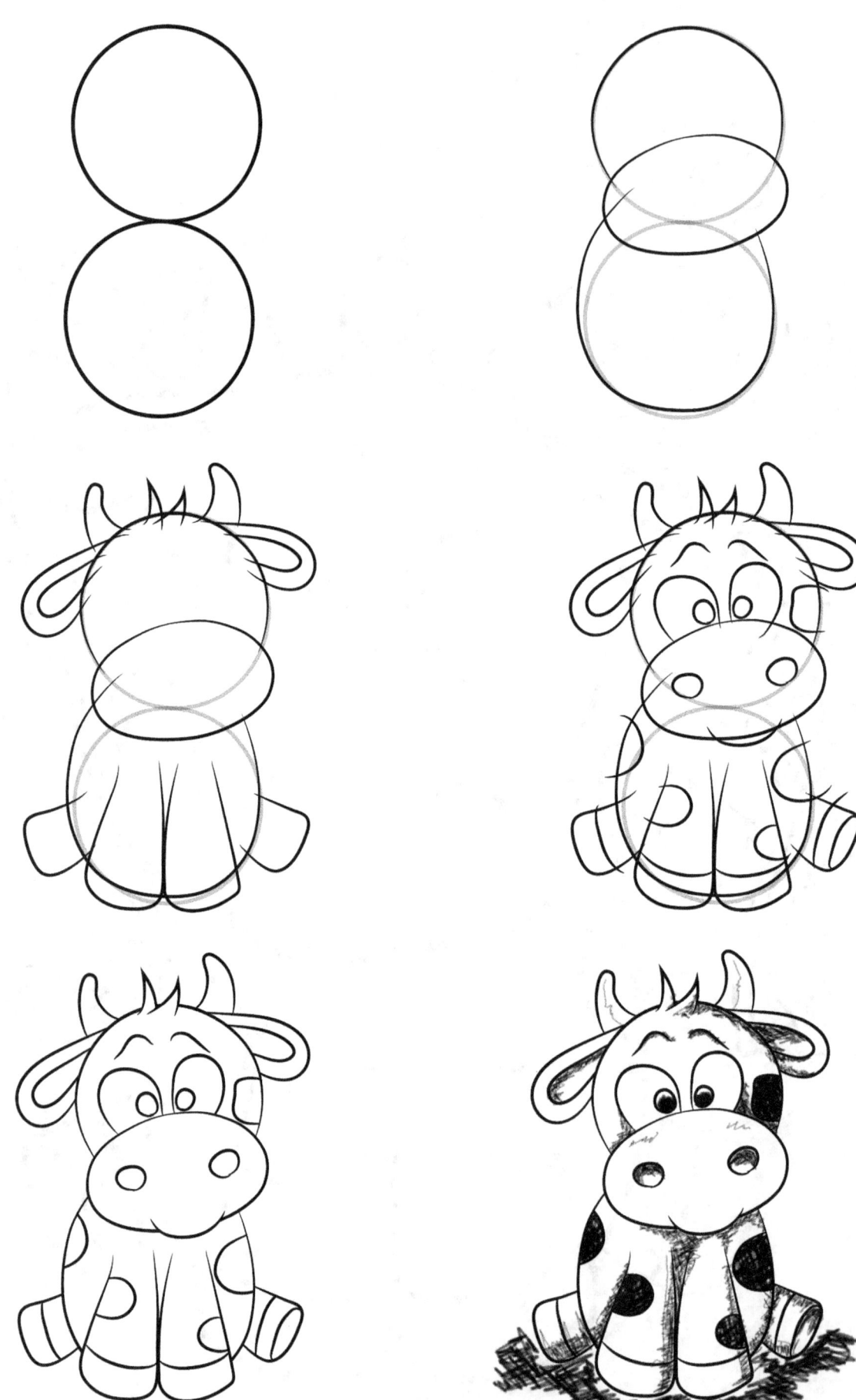

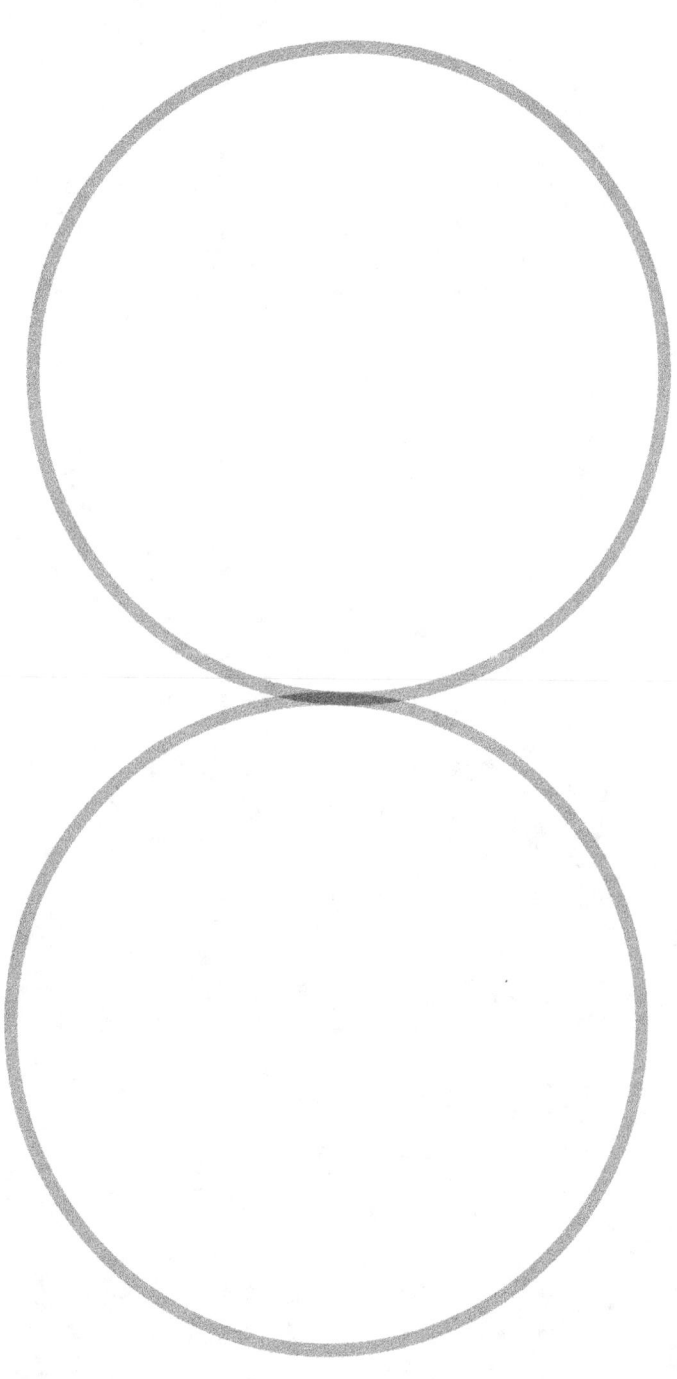

SQUIRREL
STAND

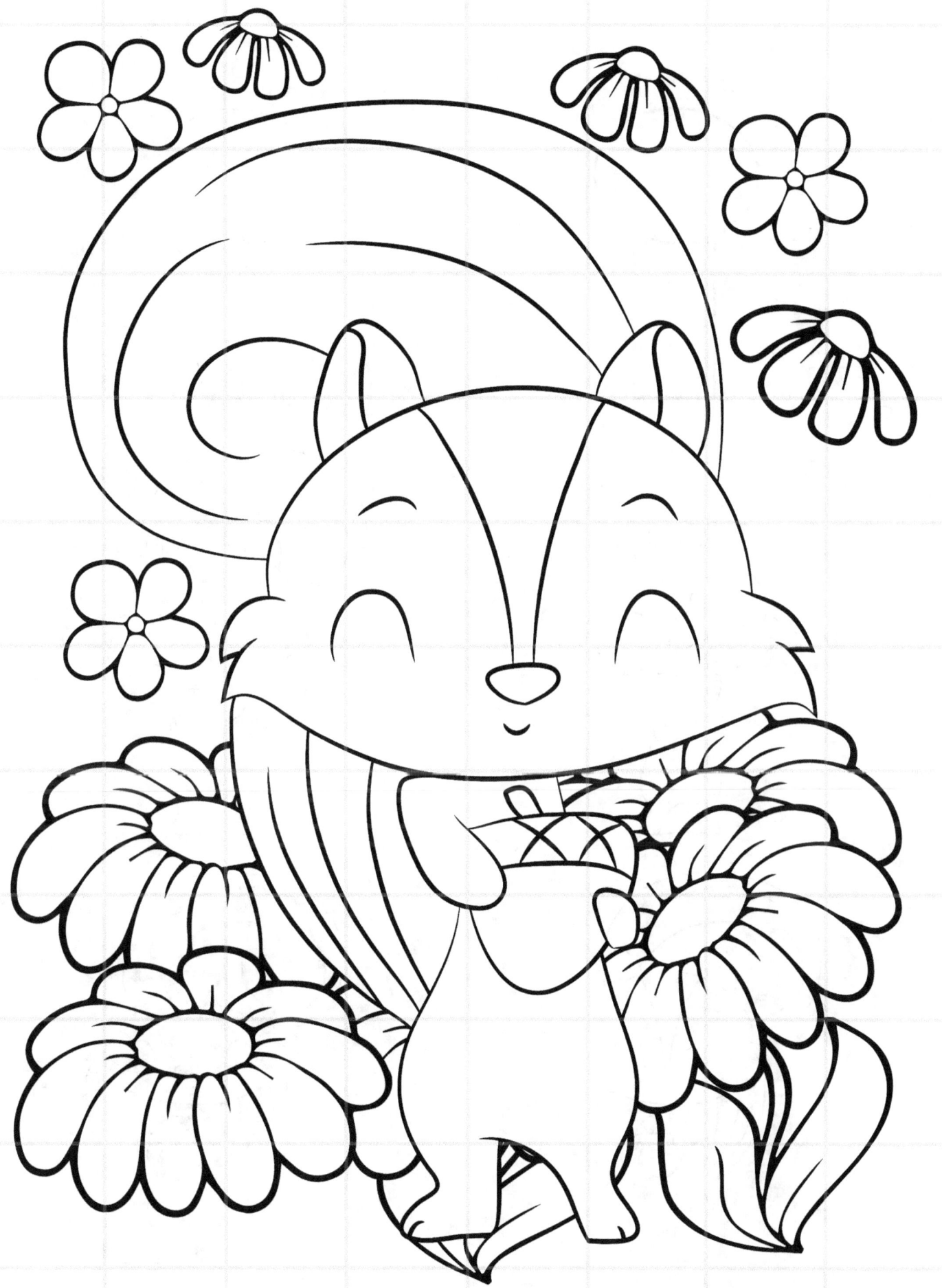

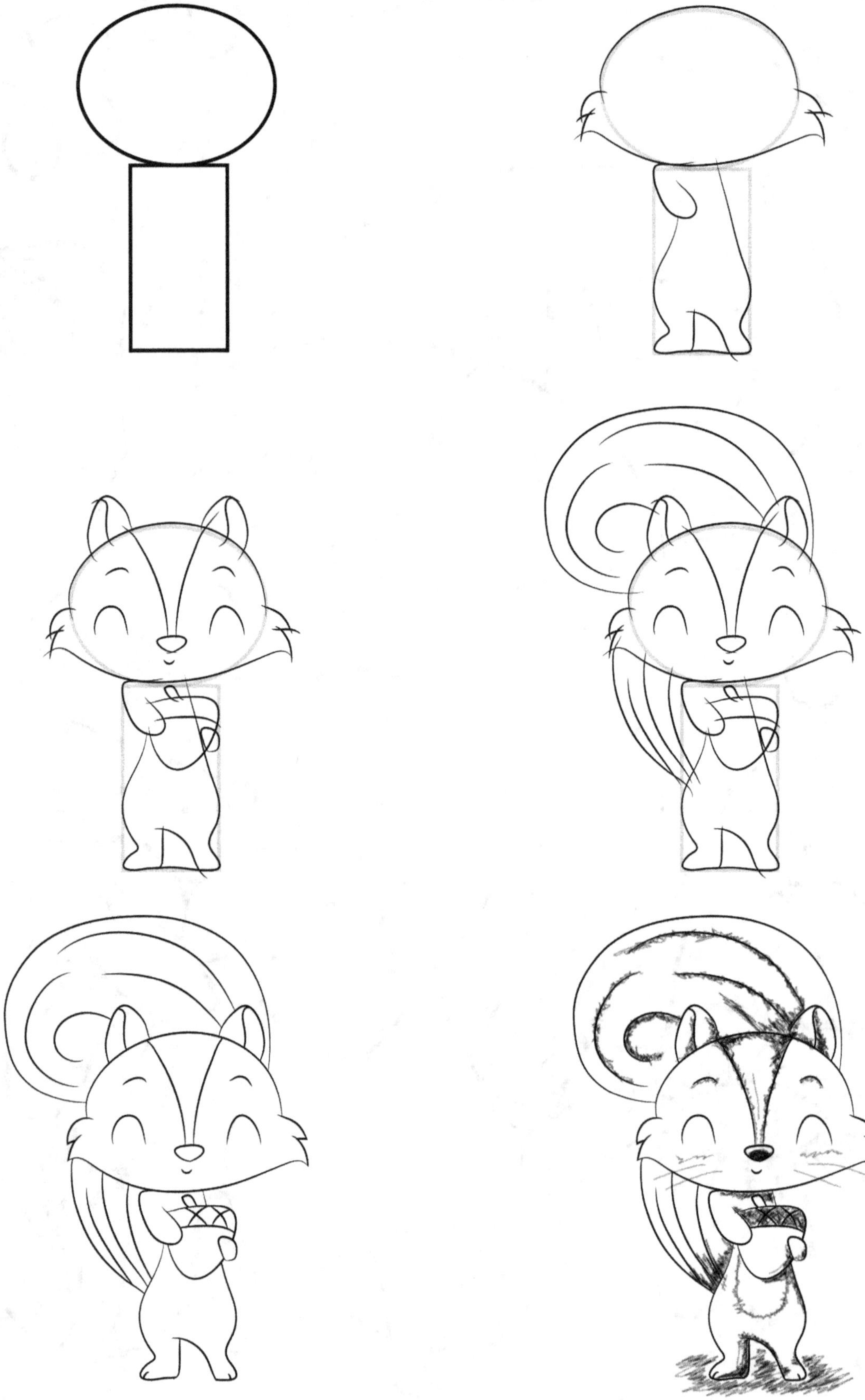

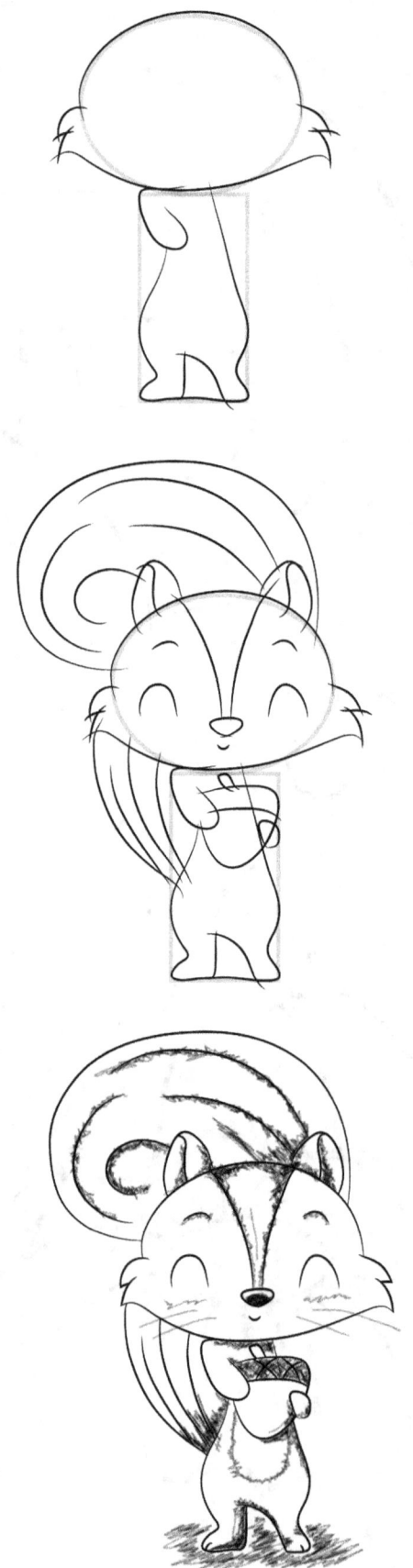

RABBIT

PLAY

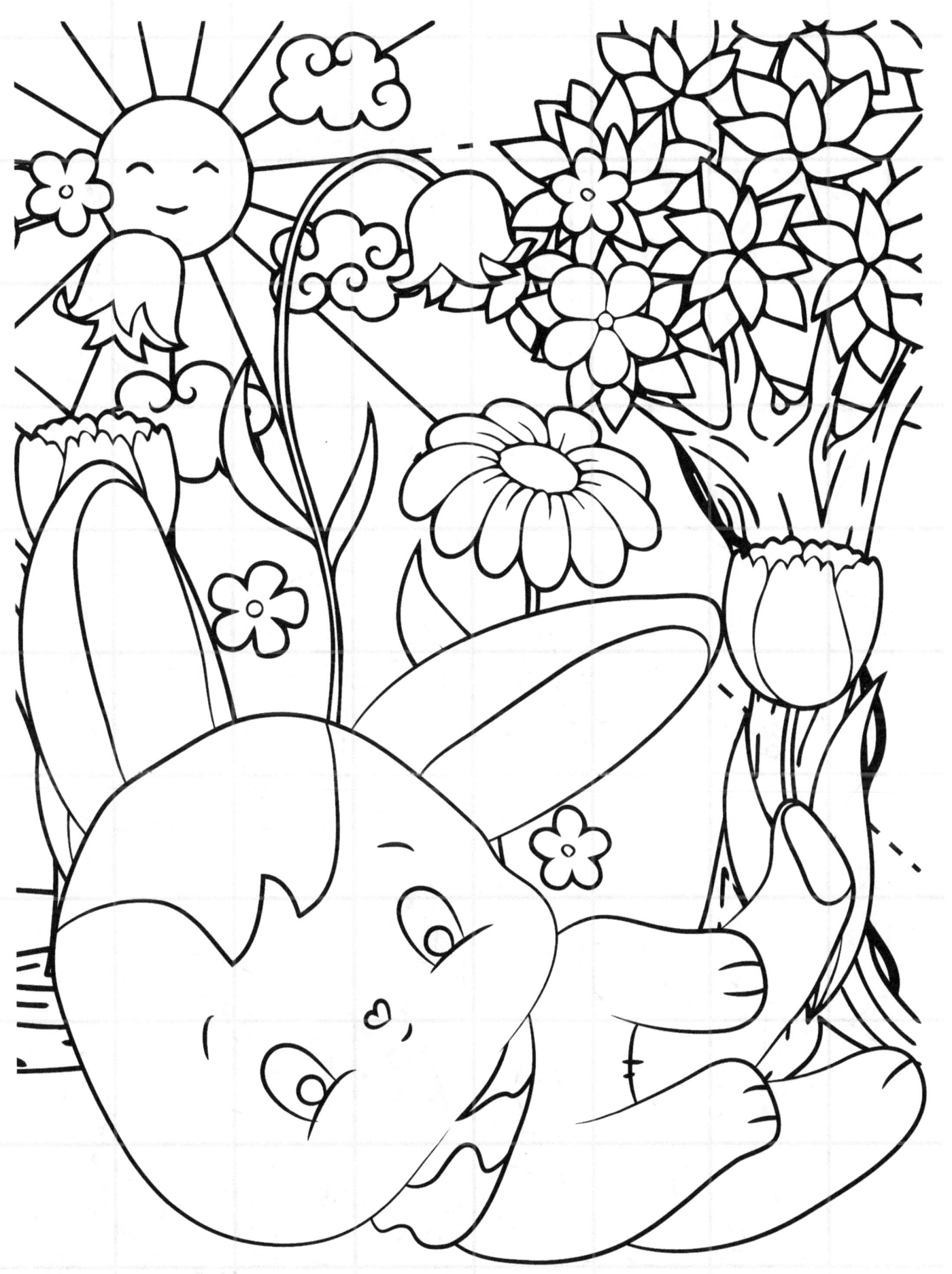

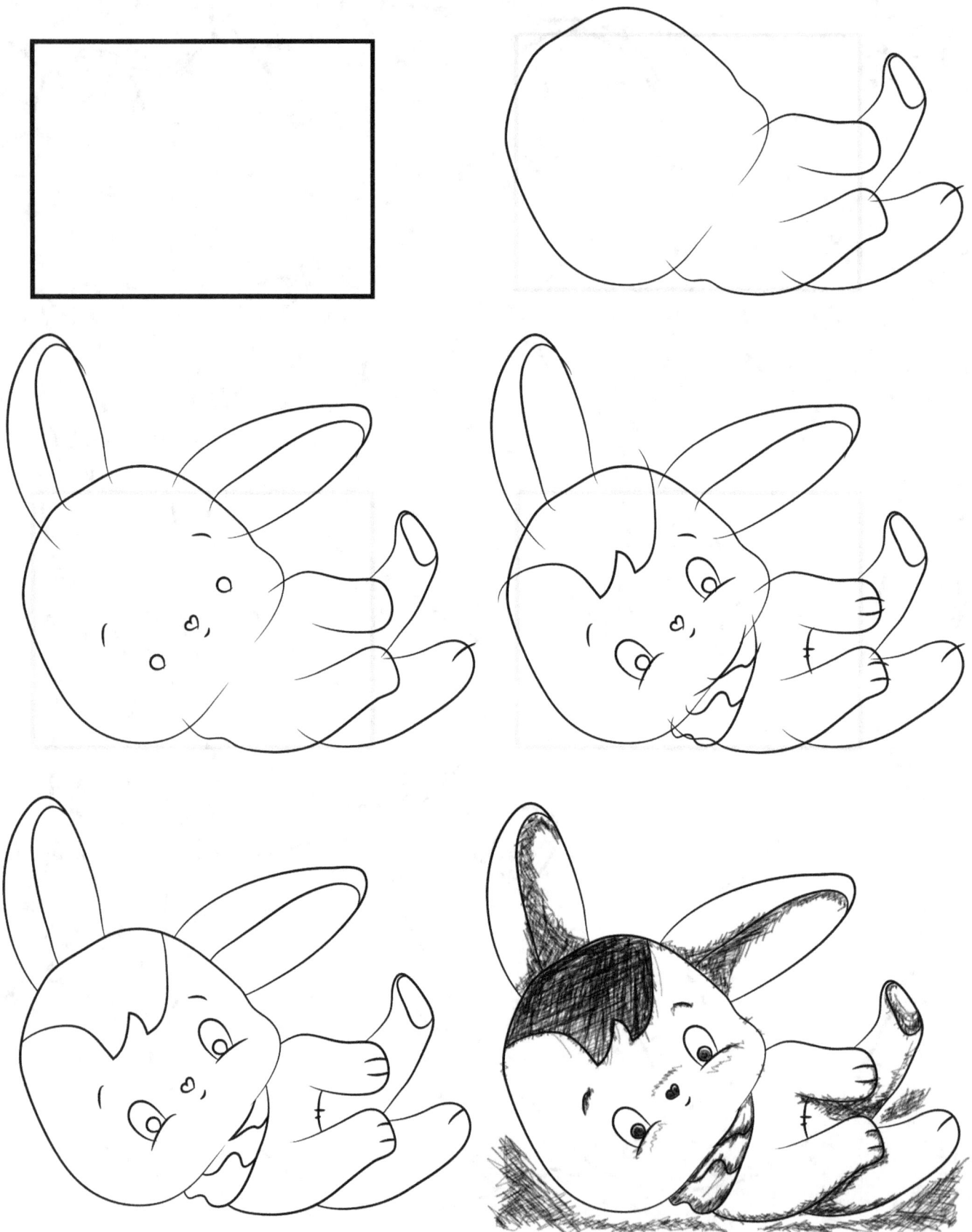

CAT

WALK

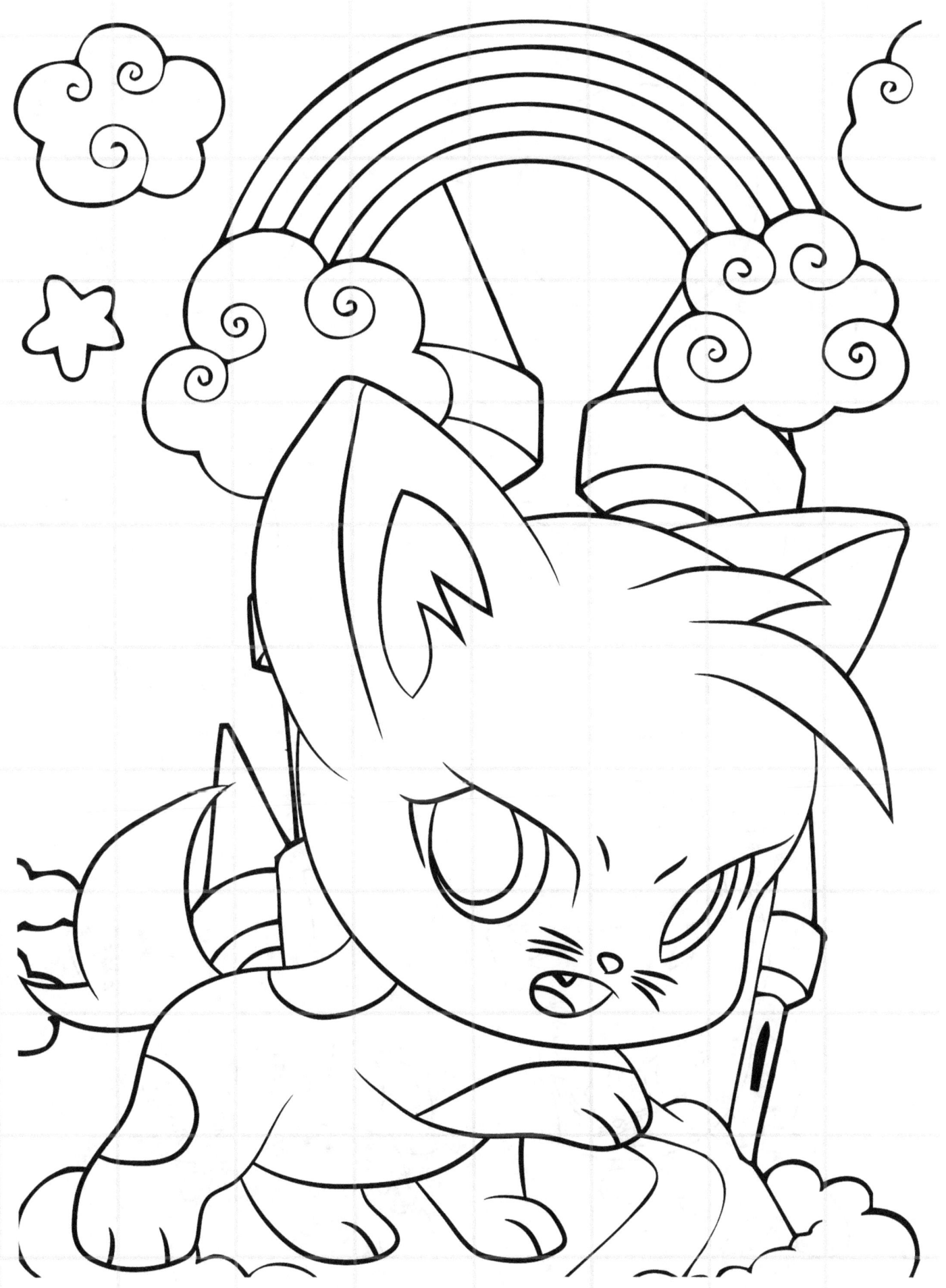

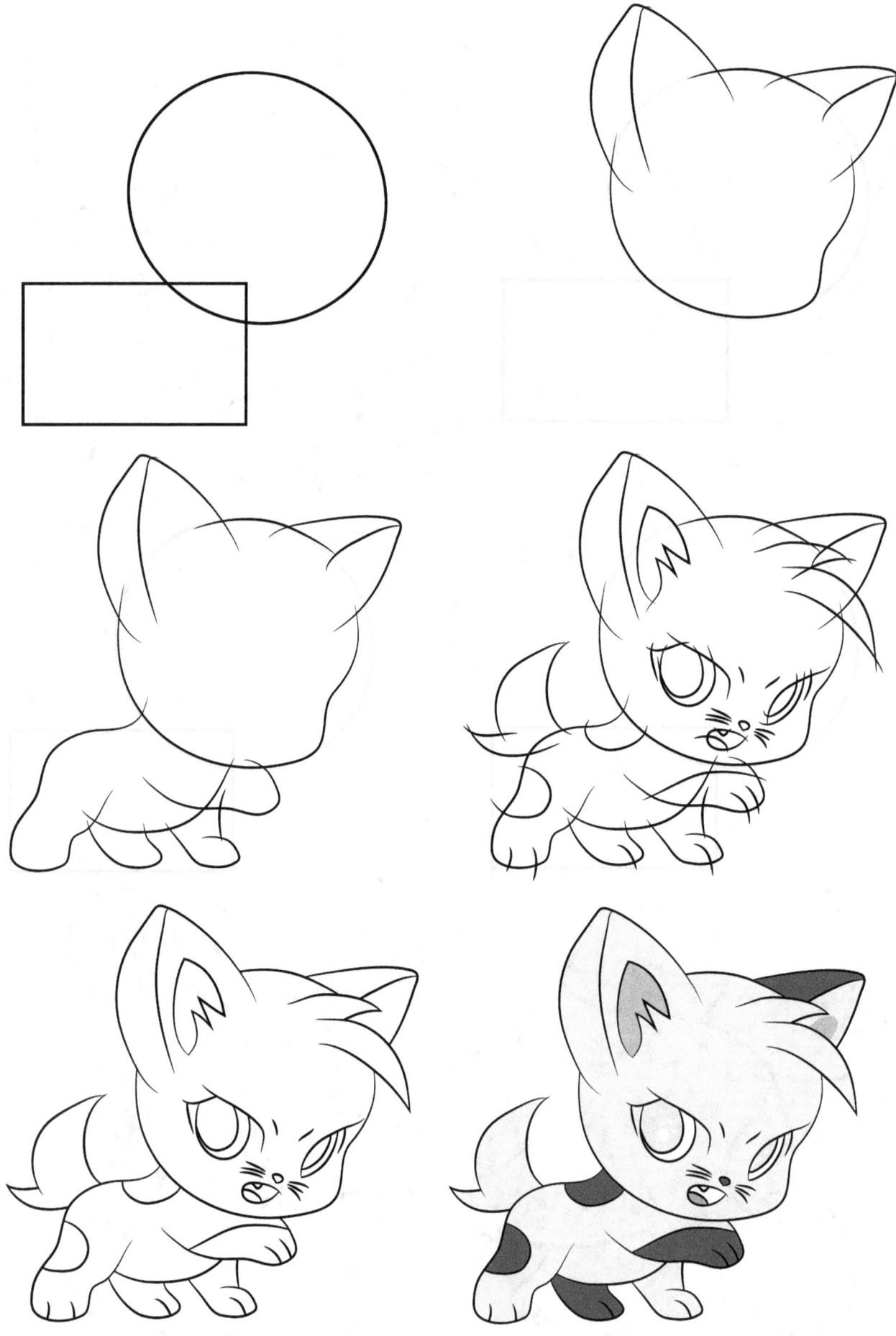

DOG

JUMP

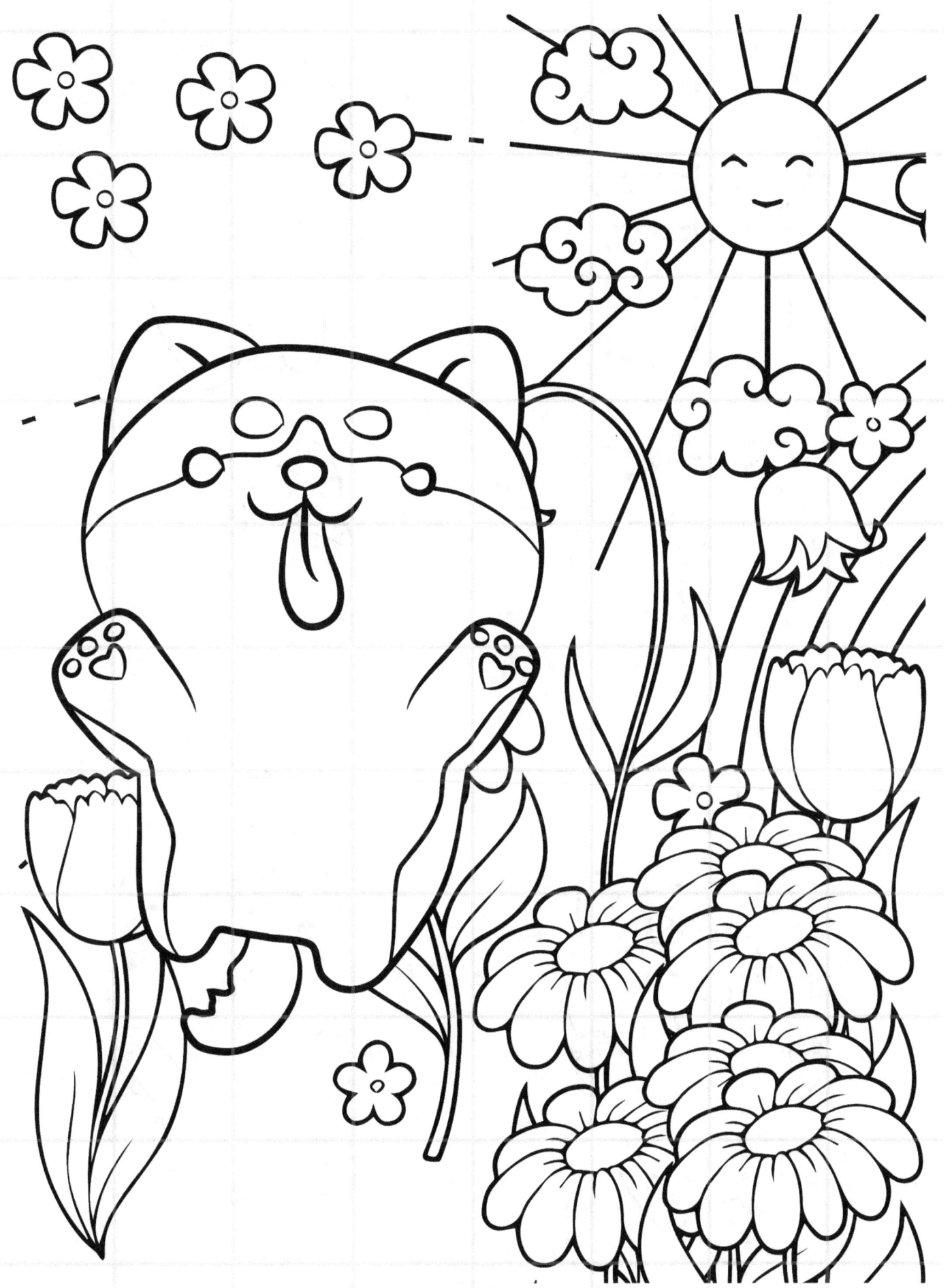

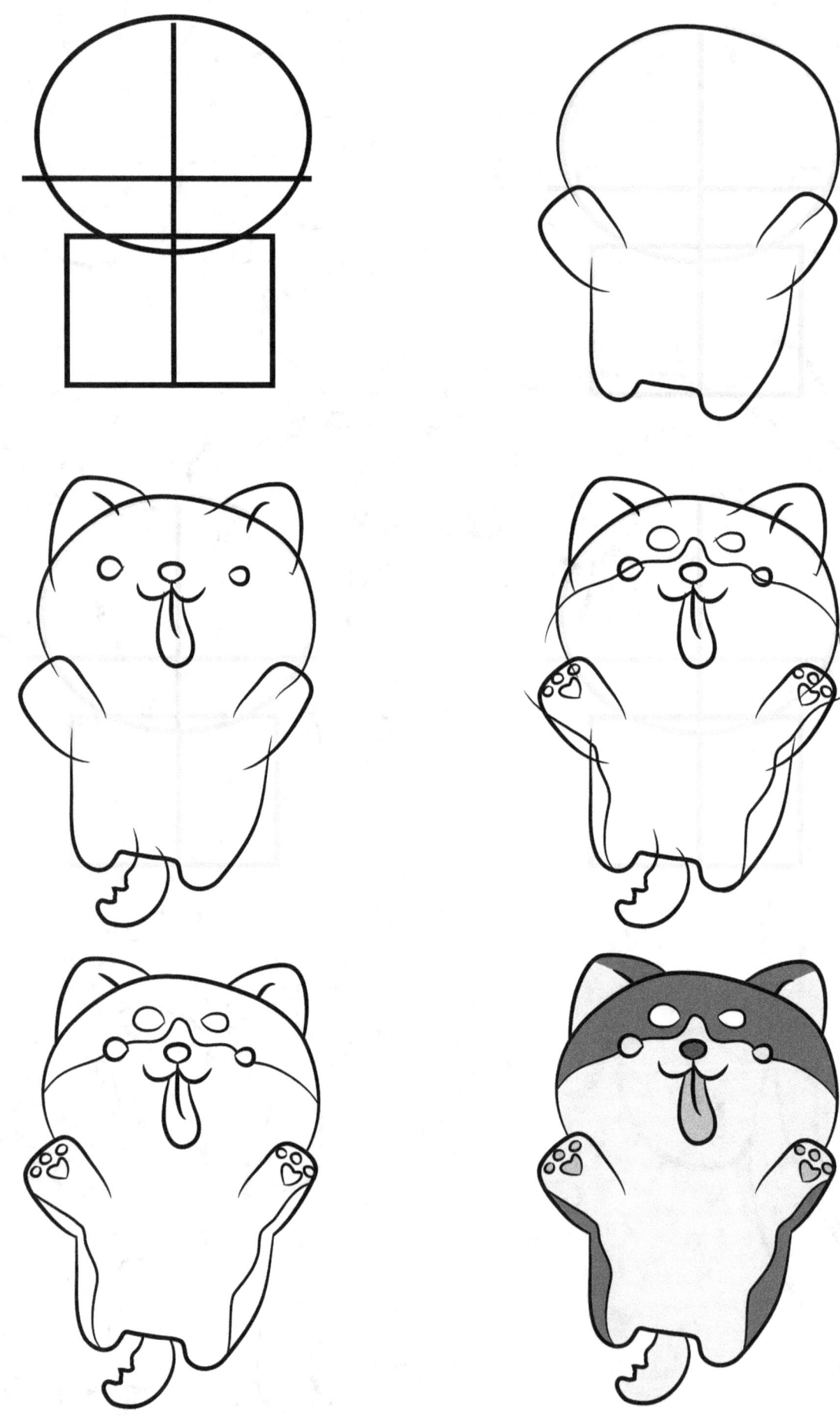

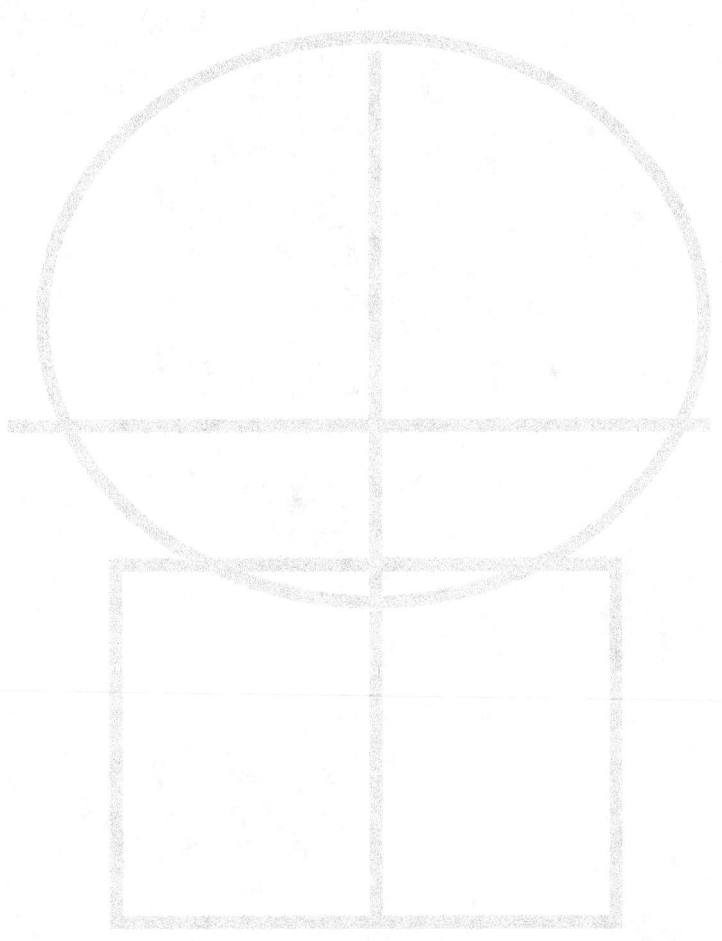

DOG

SIT

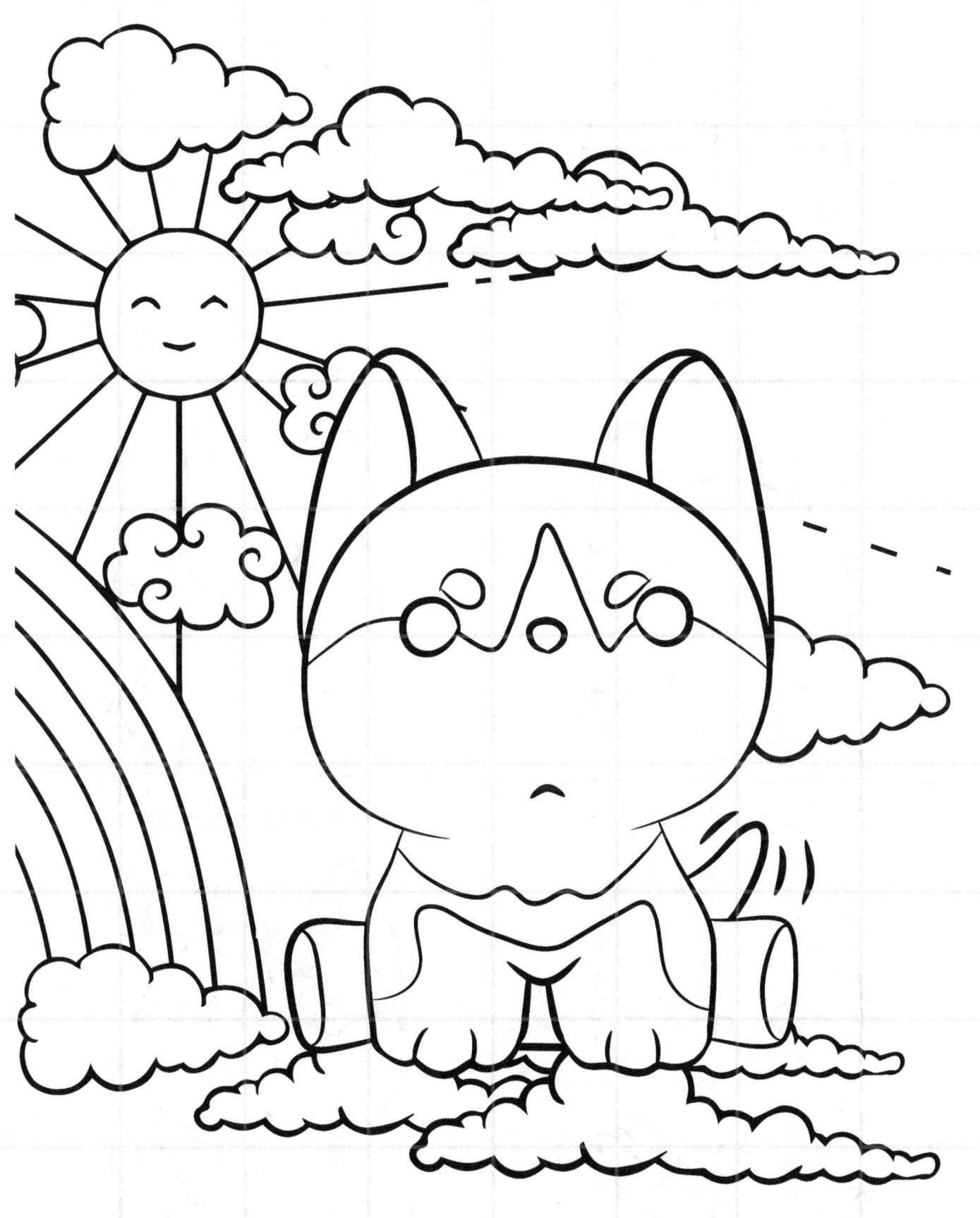

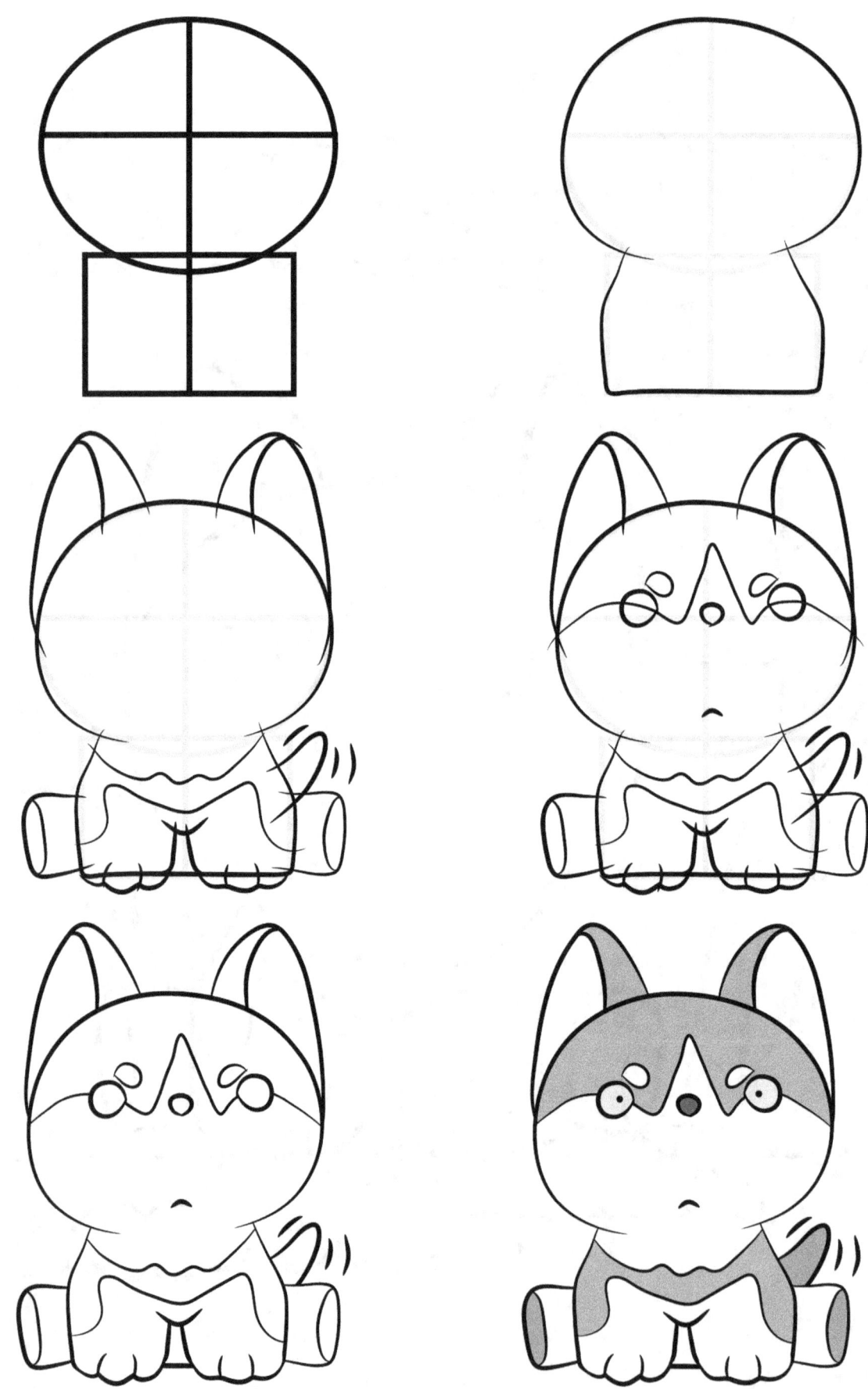

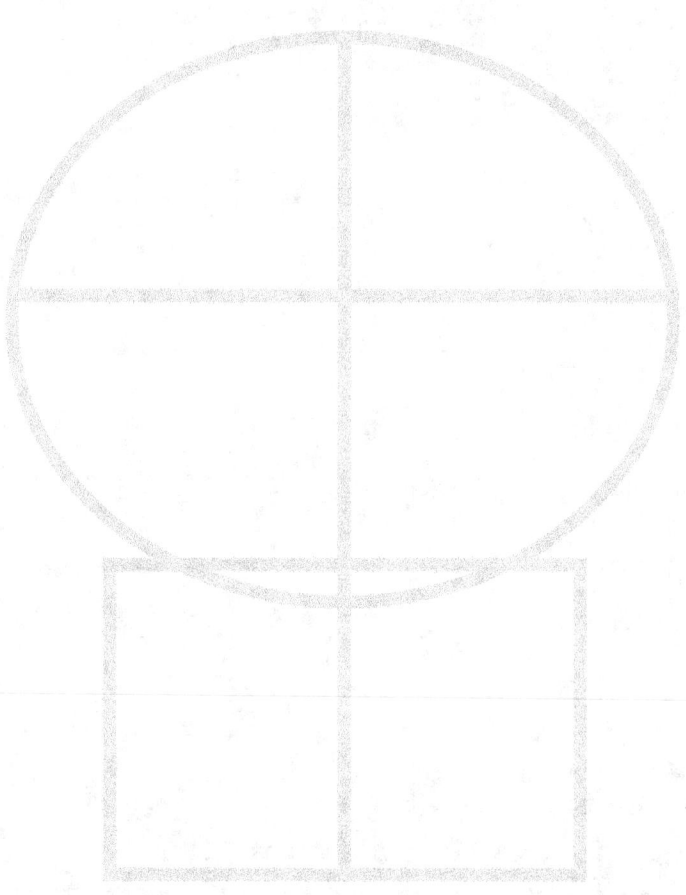

CAT

SIT

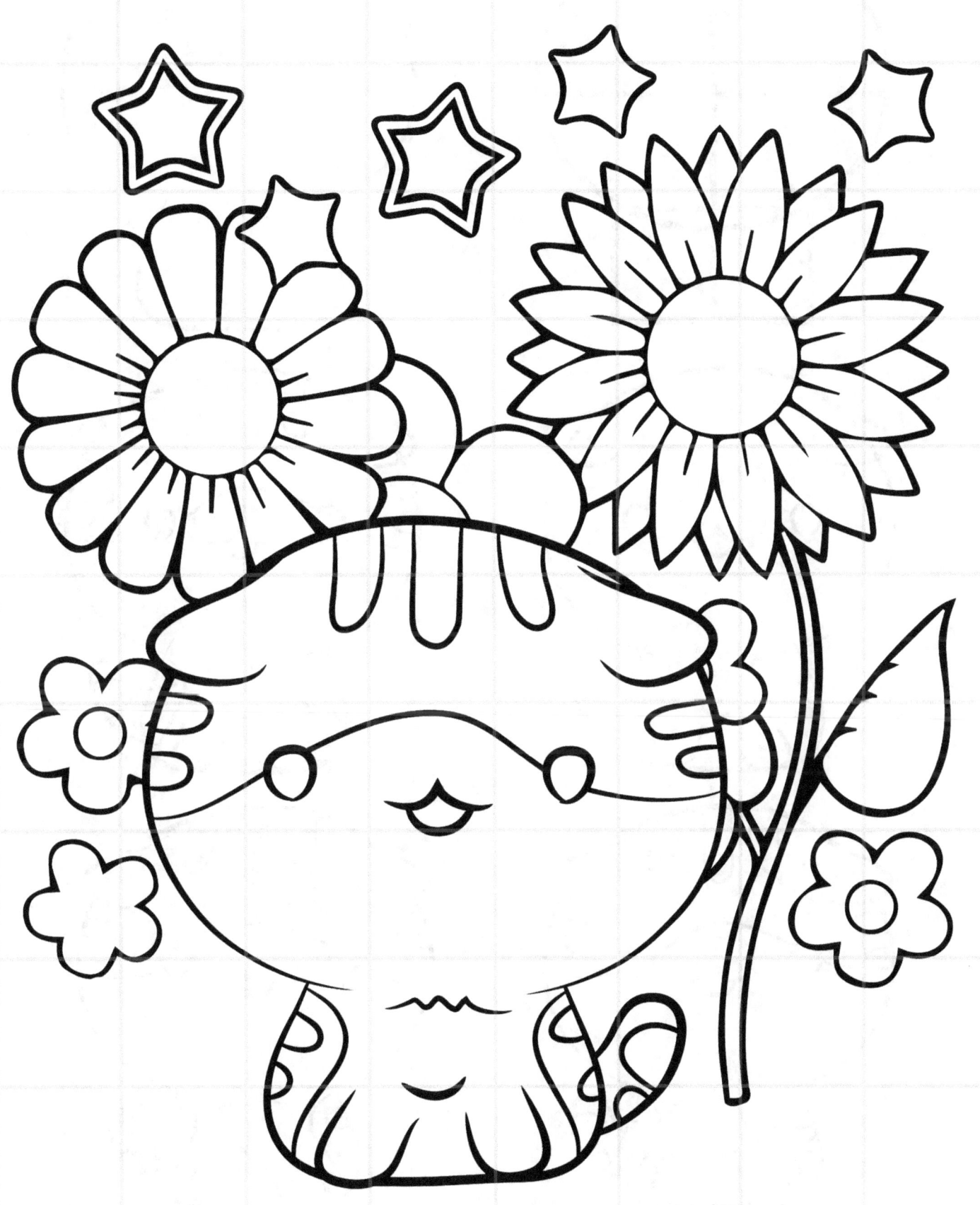

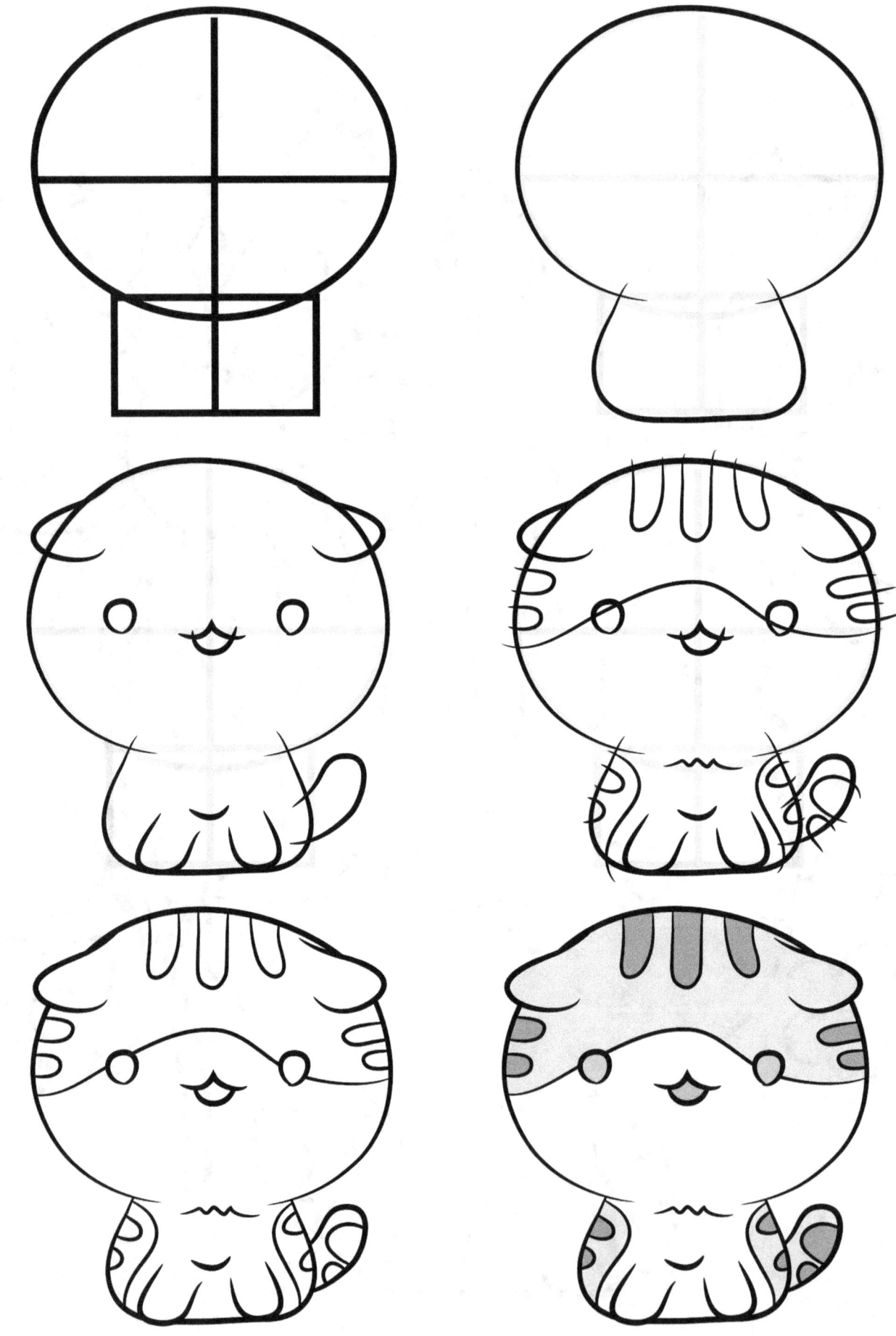

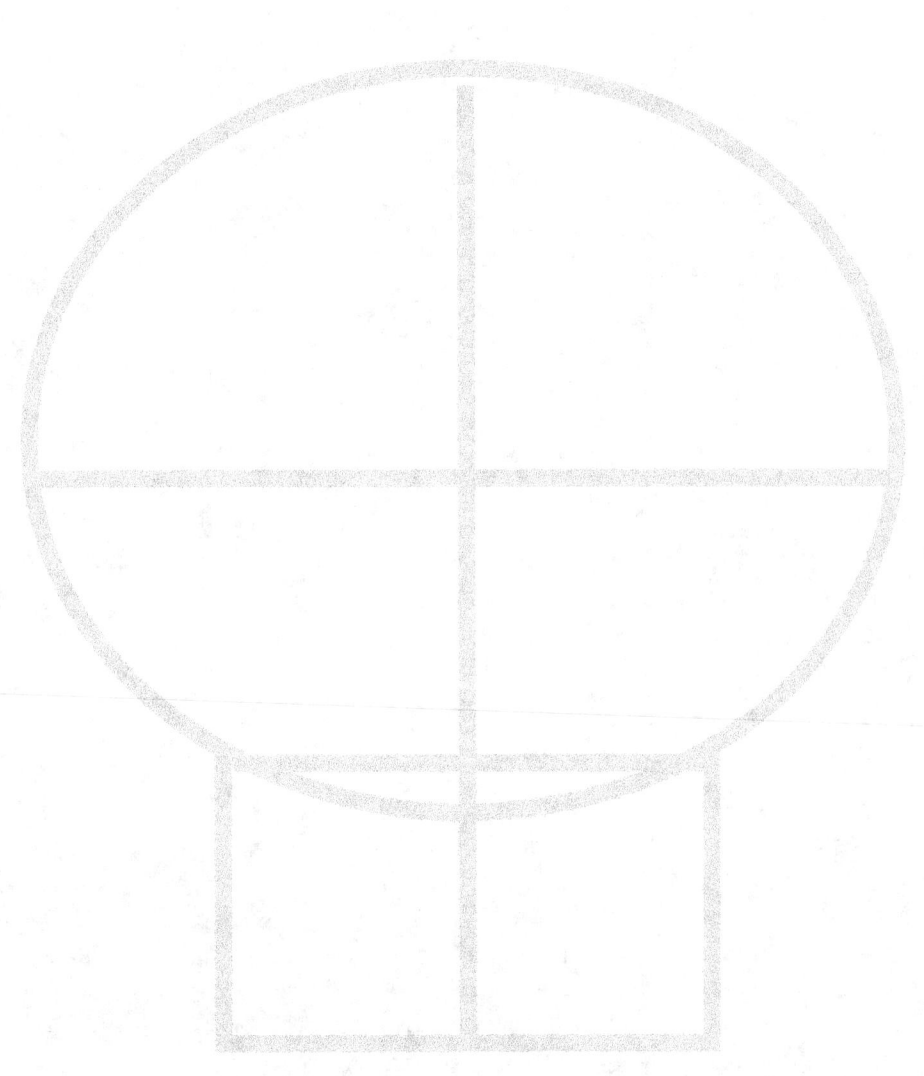

CAT

SIT

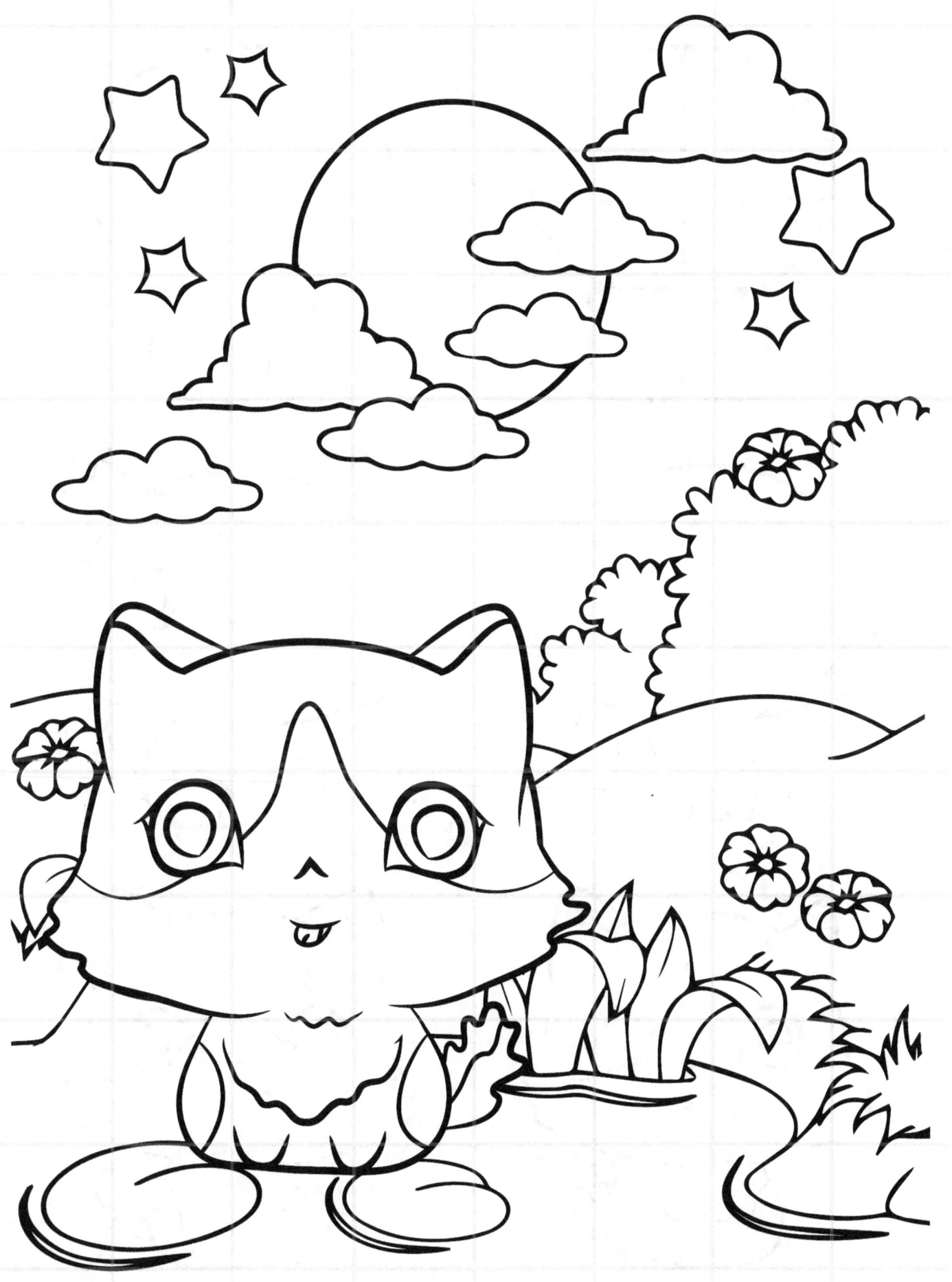

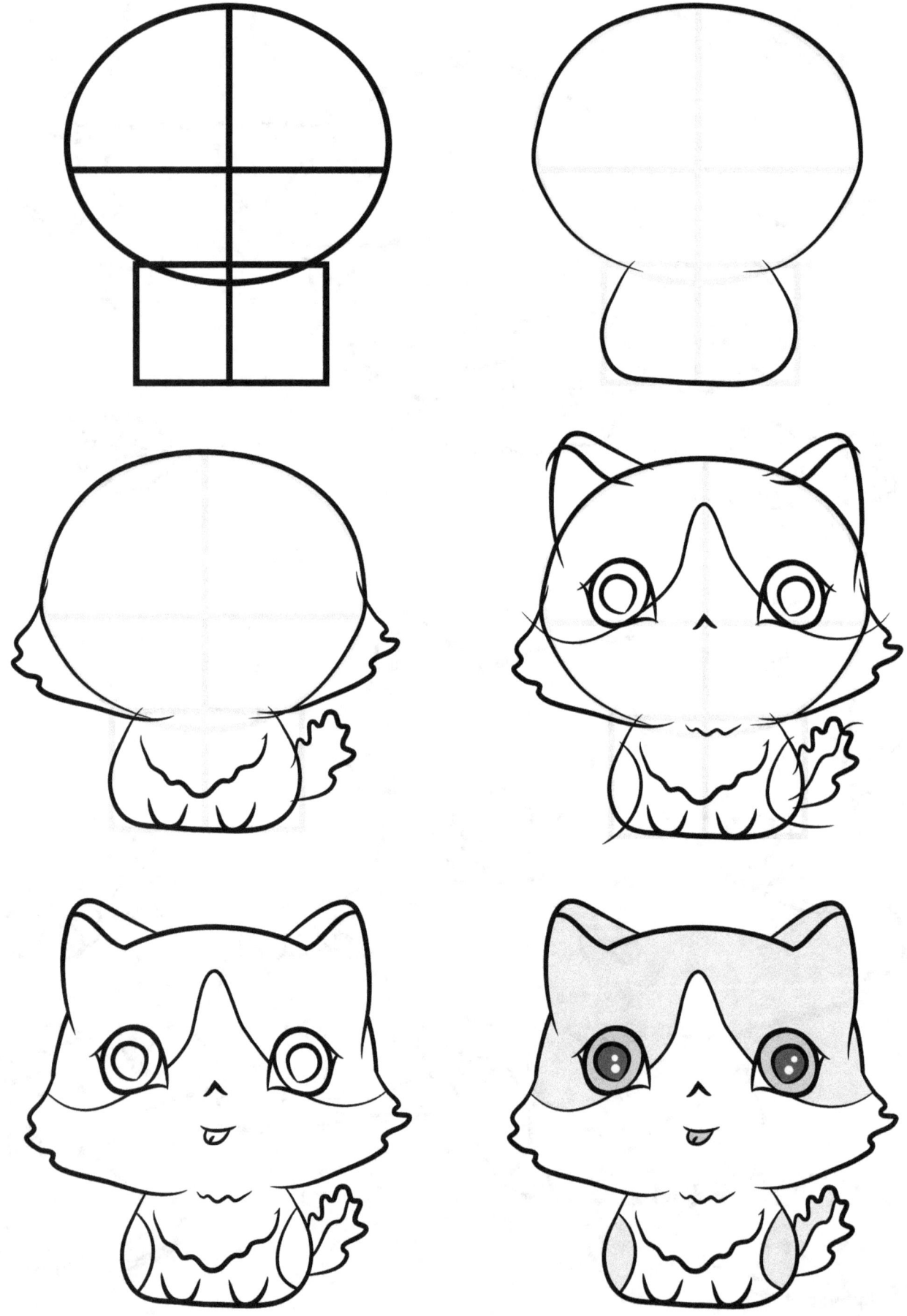

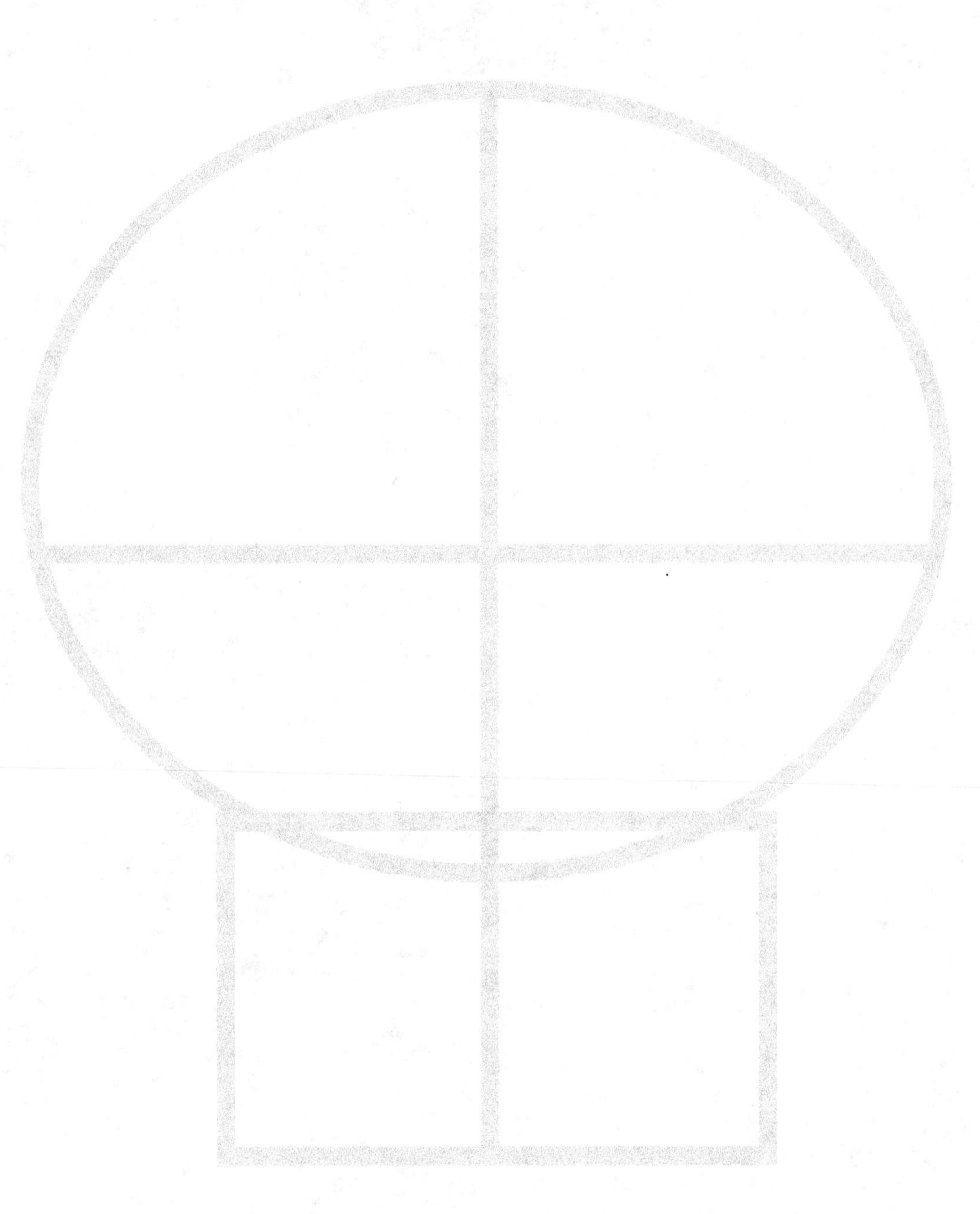

WHALE
PLAY

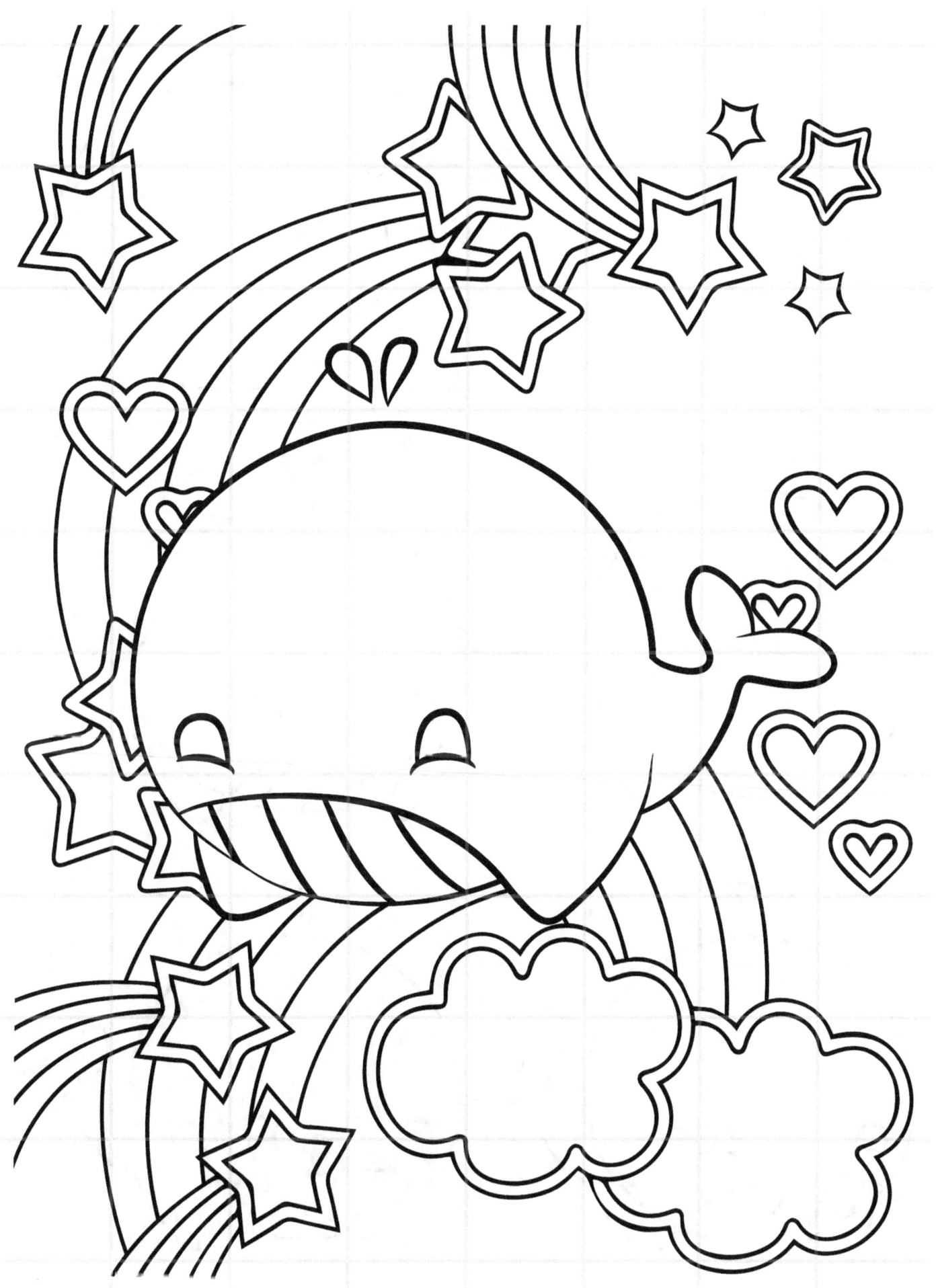

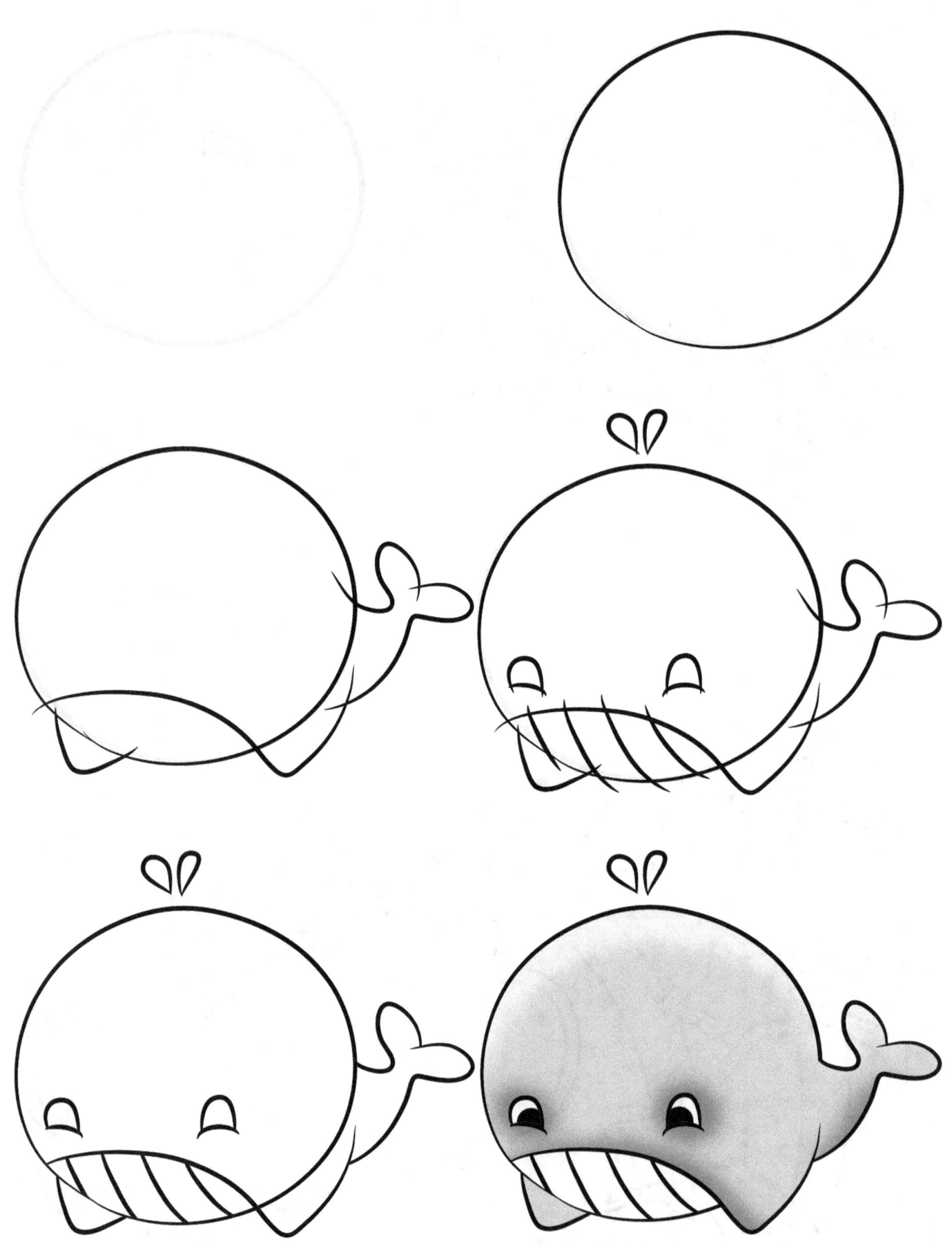

FOX

STAND

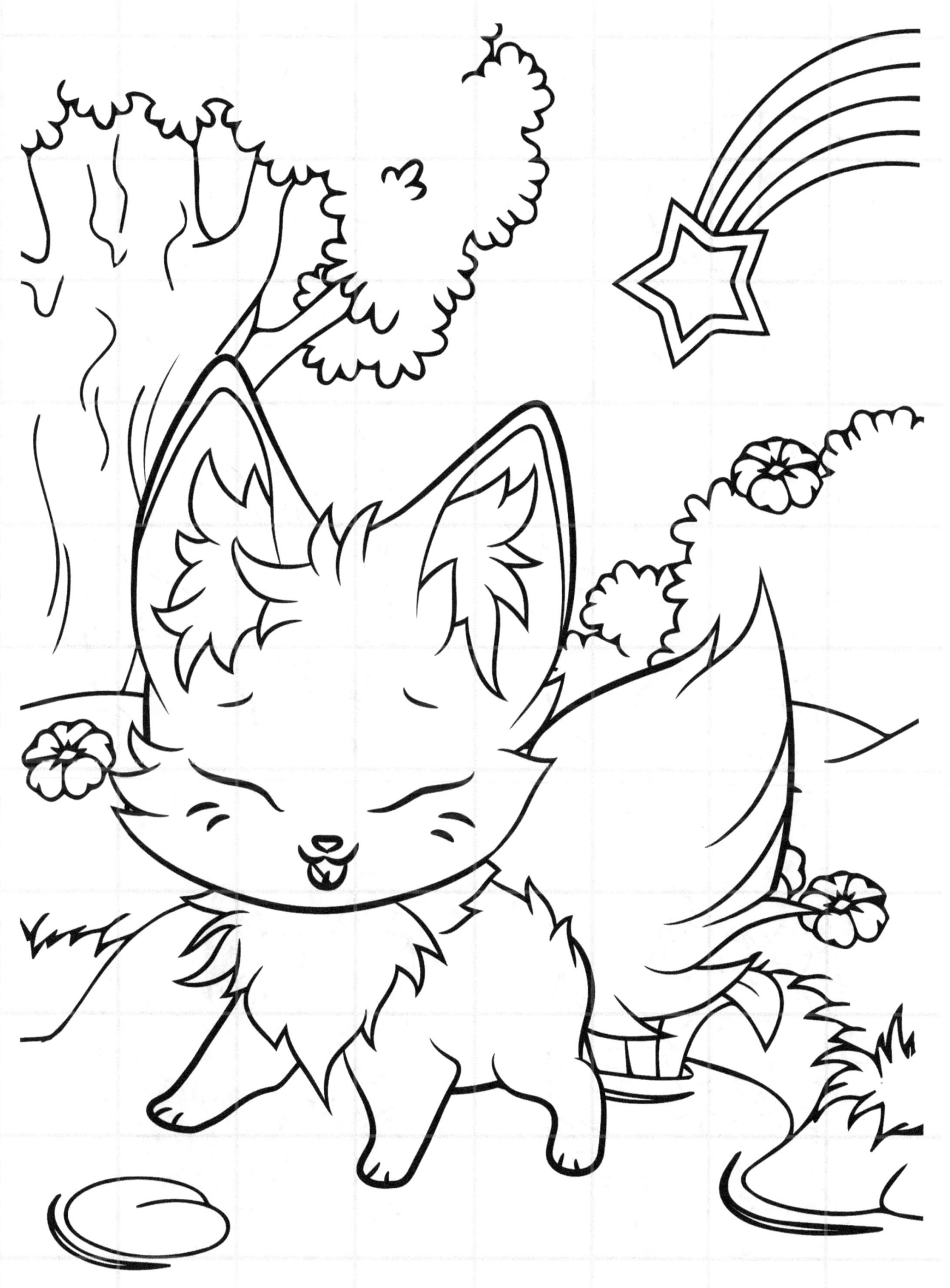

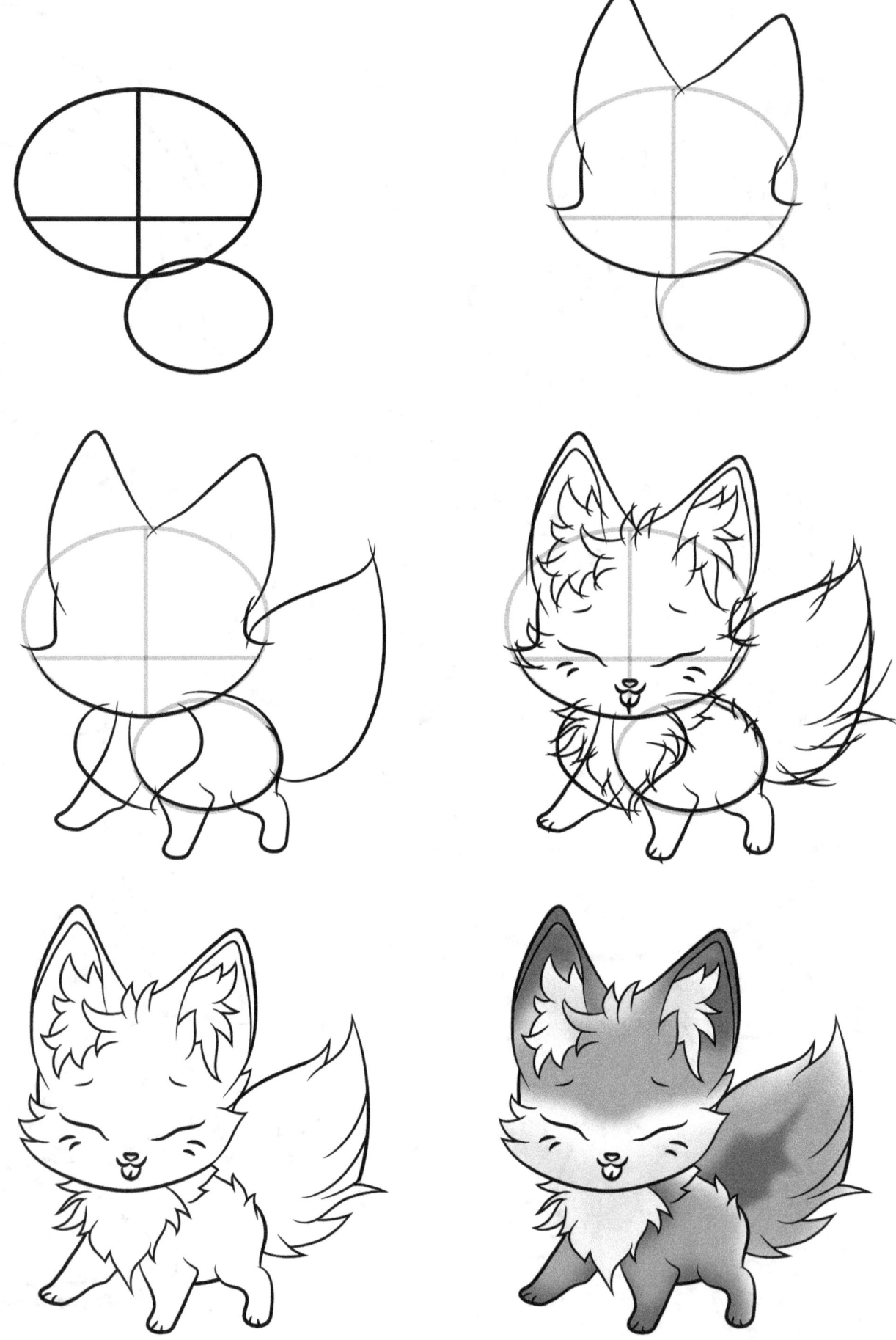

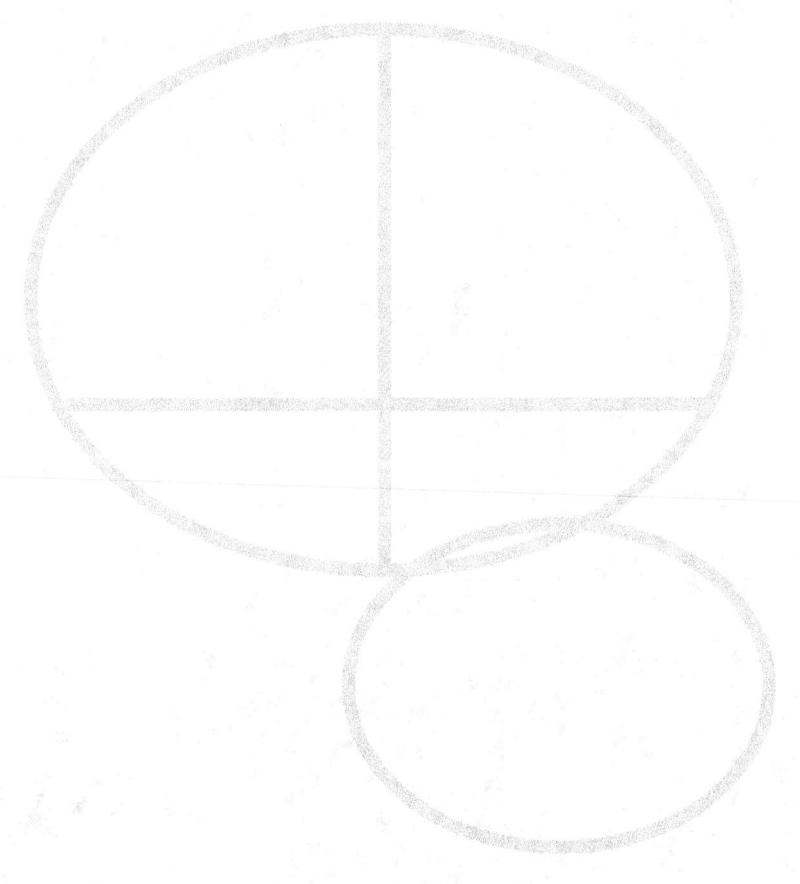

FOX

SIT

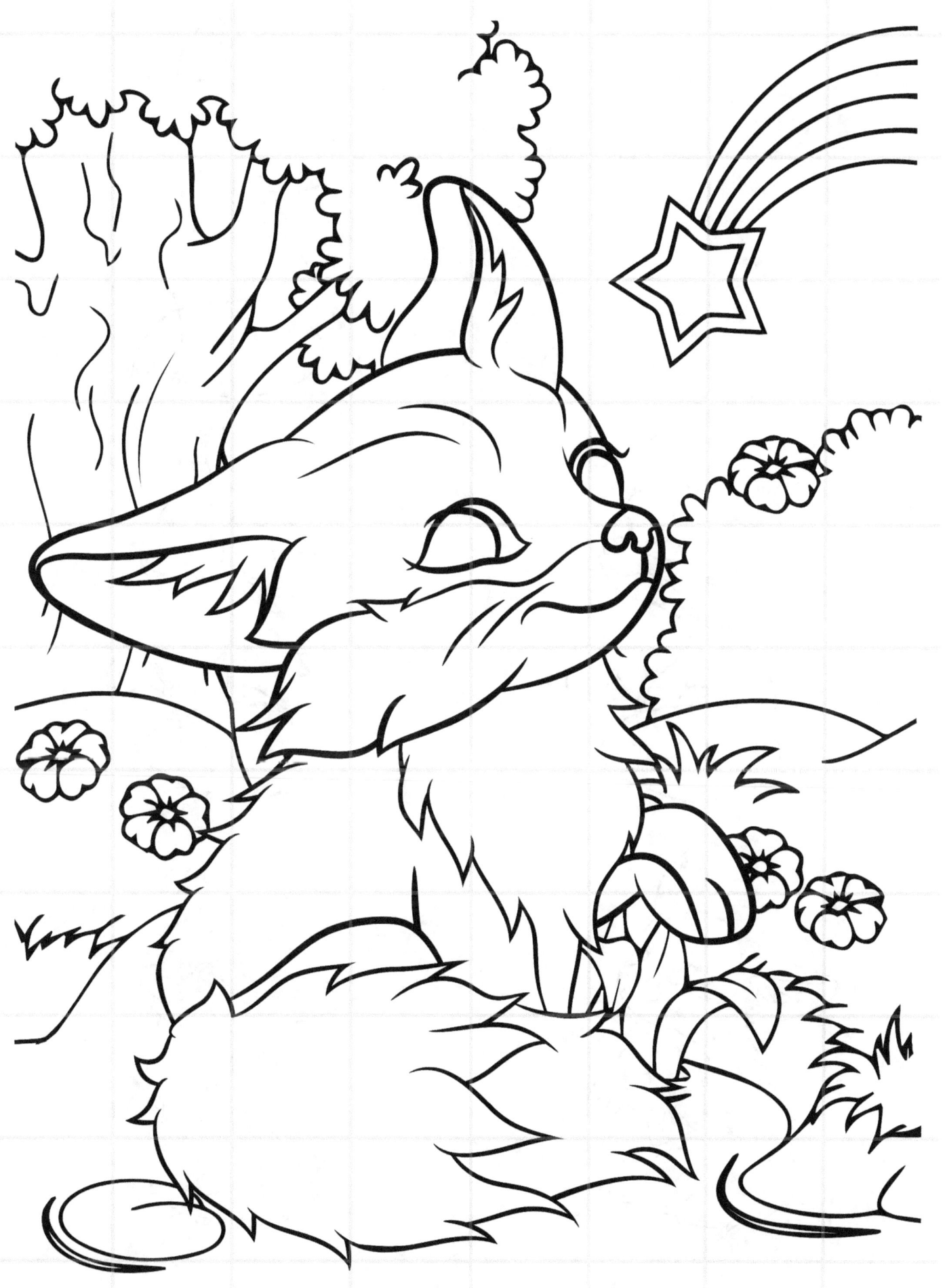

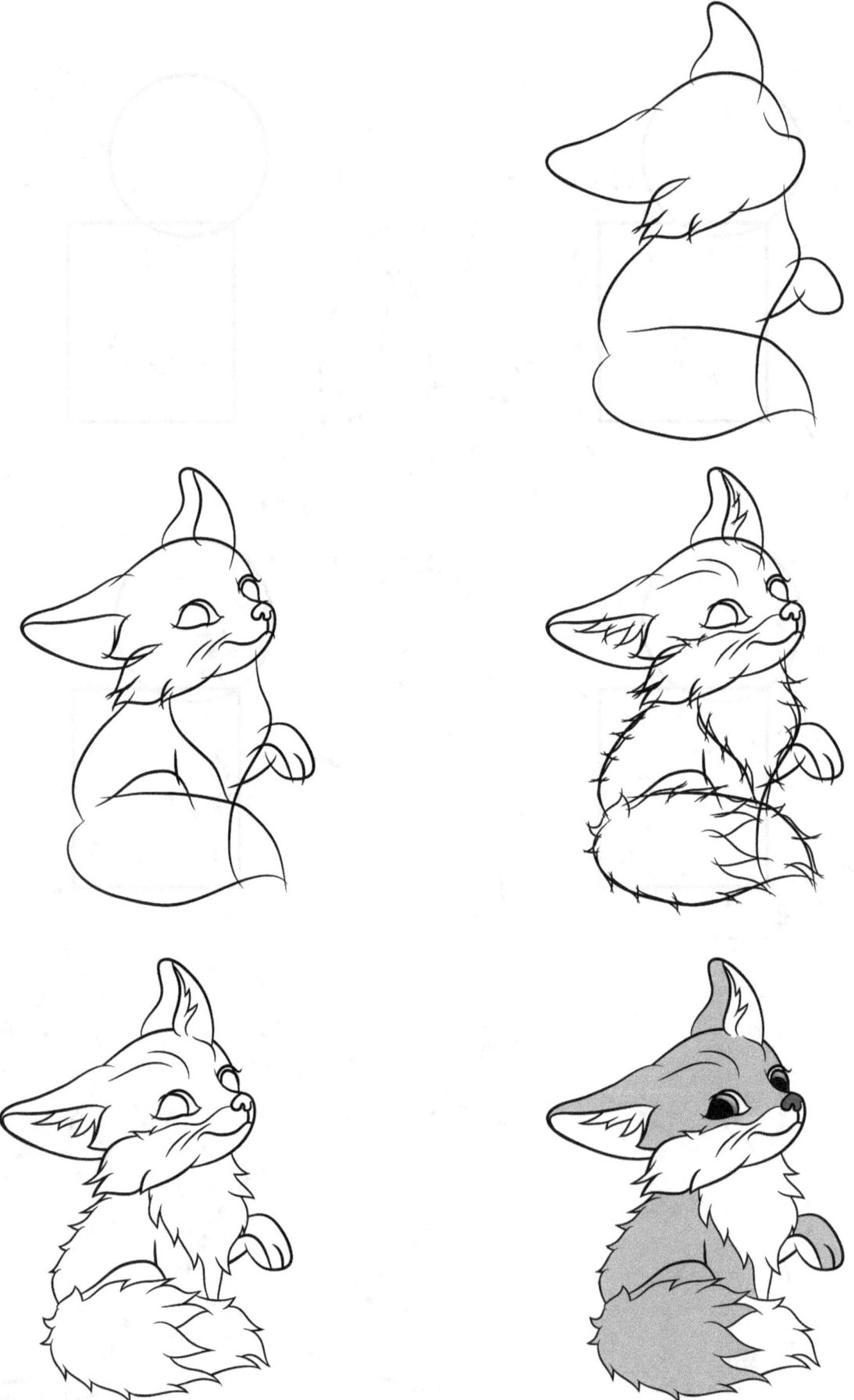

PENGUIN

STAND

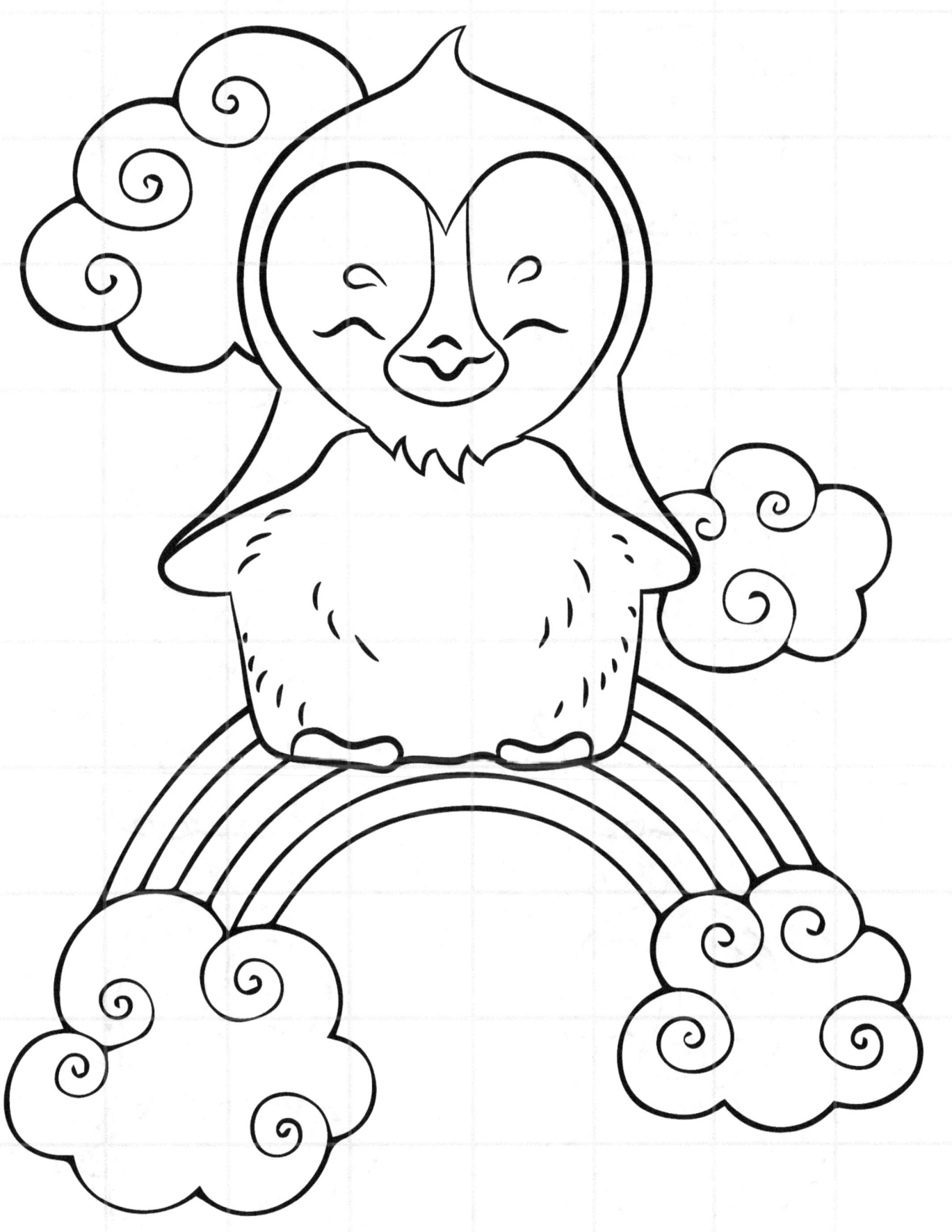

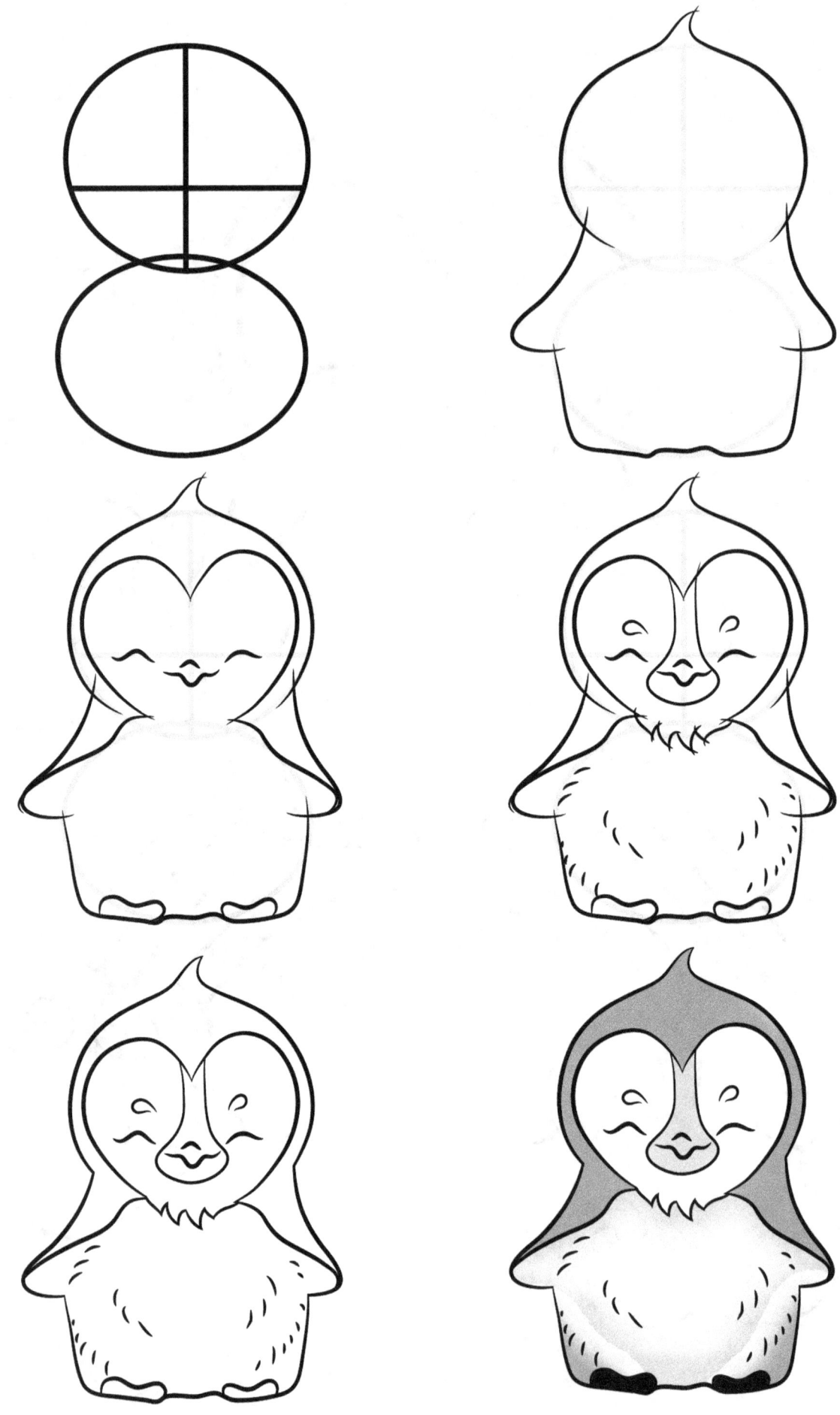

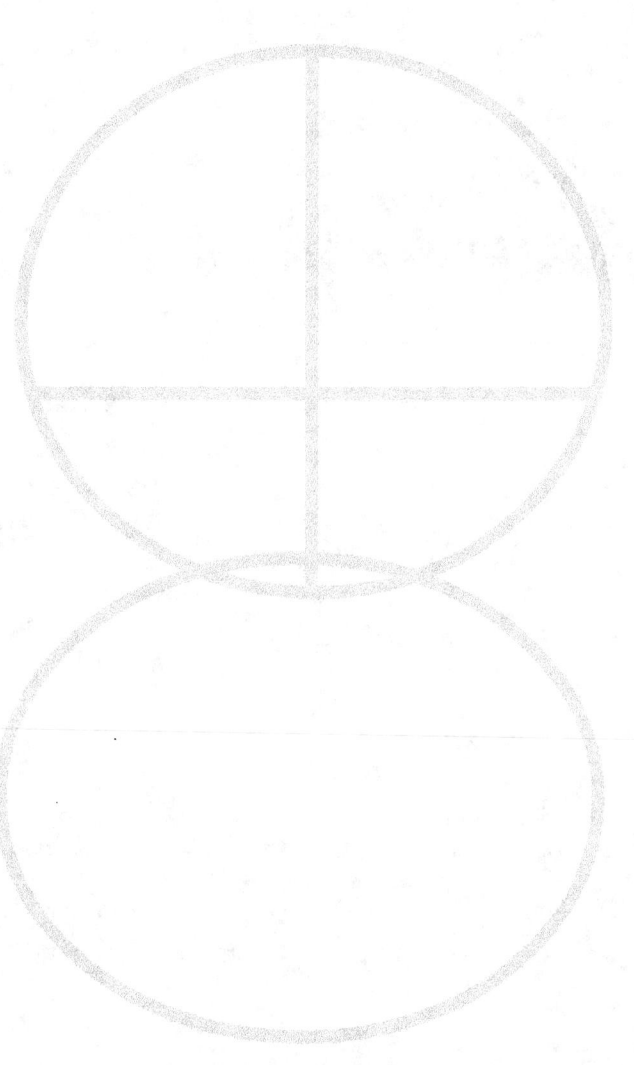

BEAR

PLAY

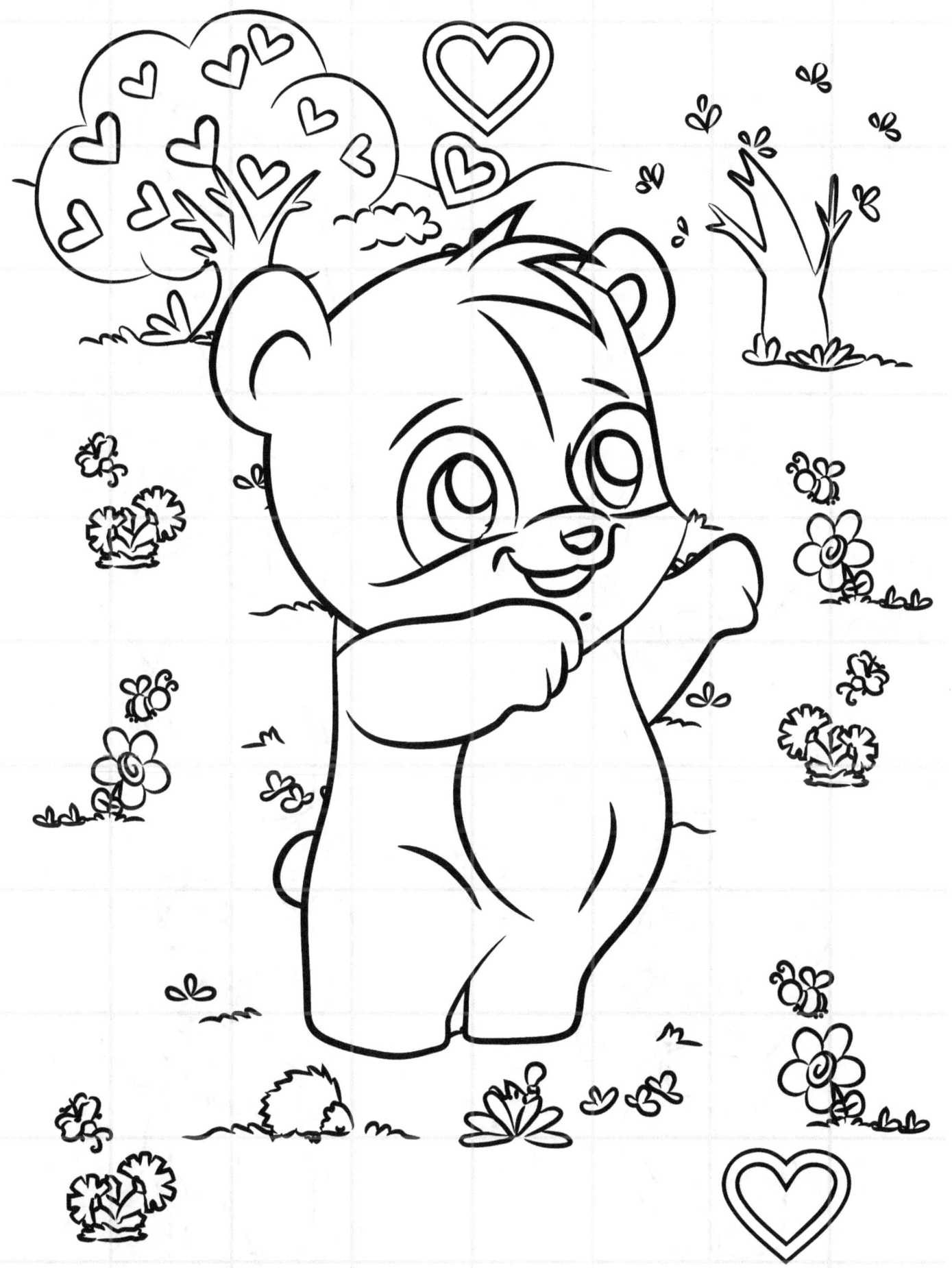

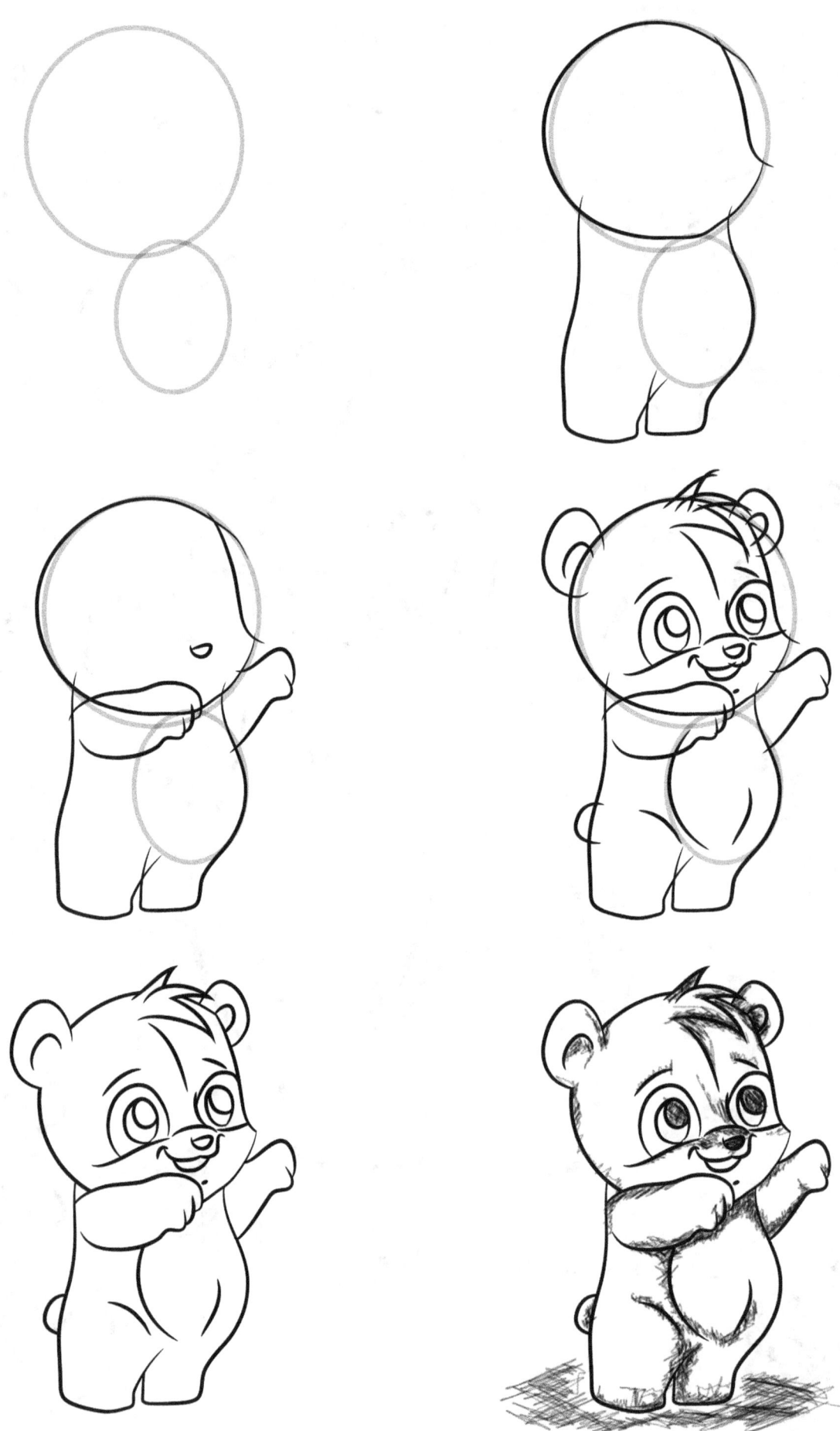

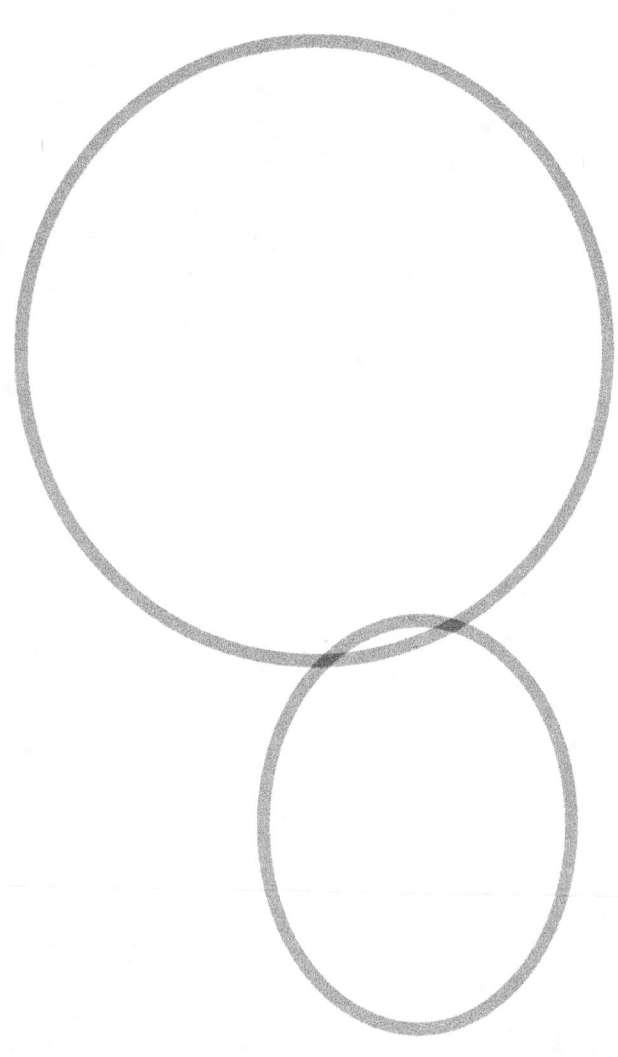

UNICORN

SIT

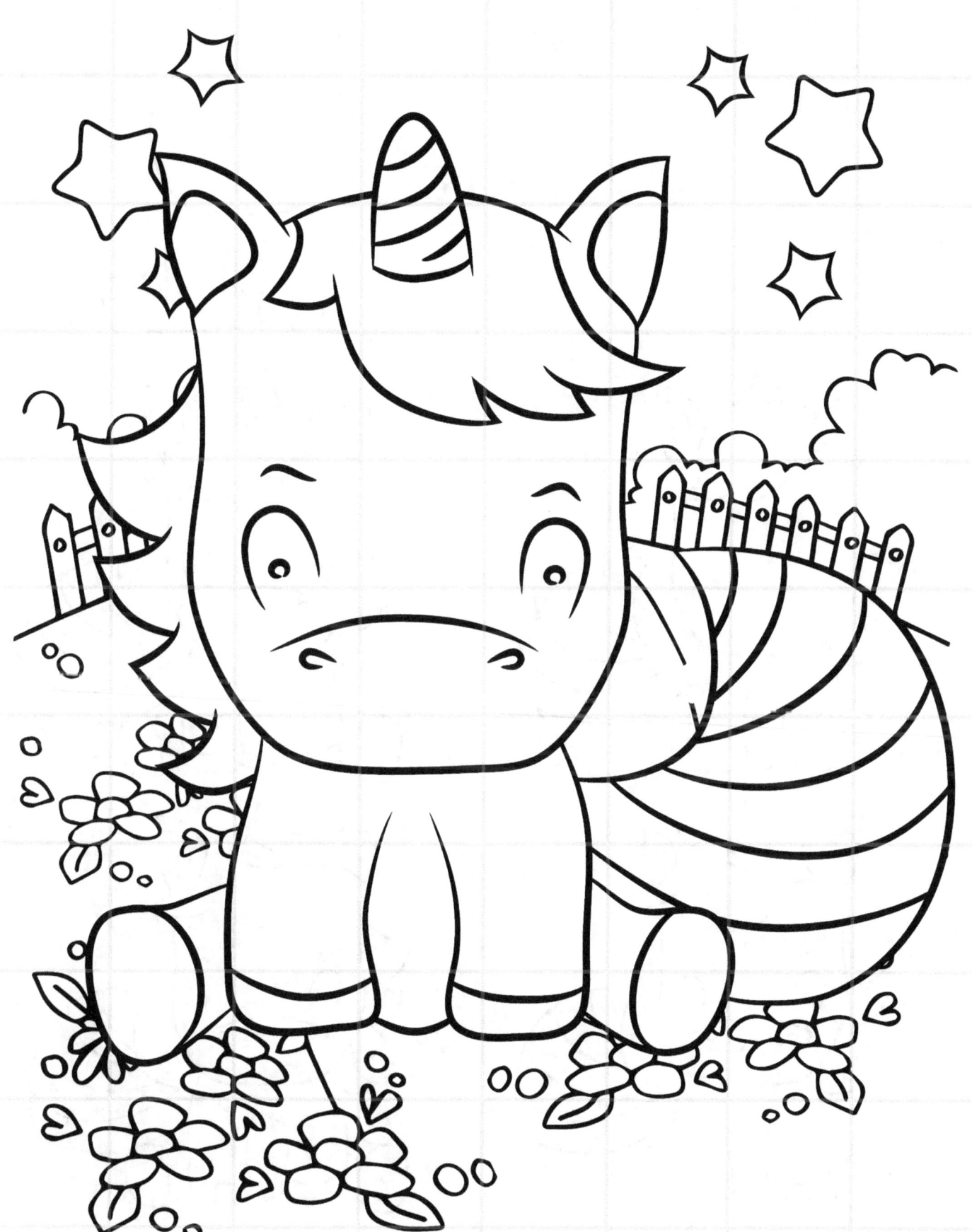

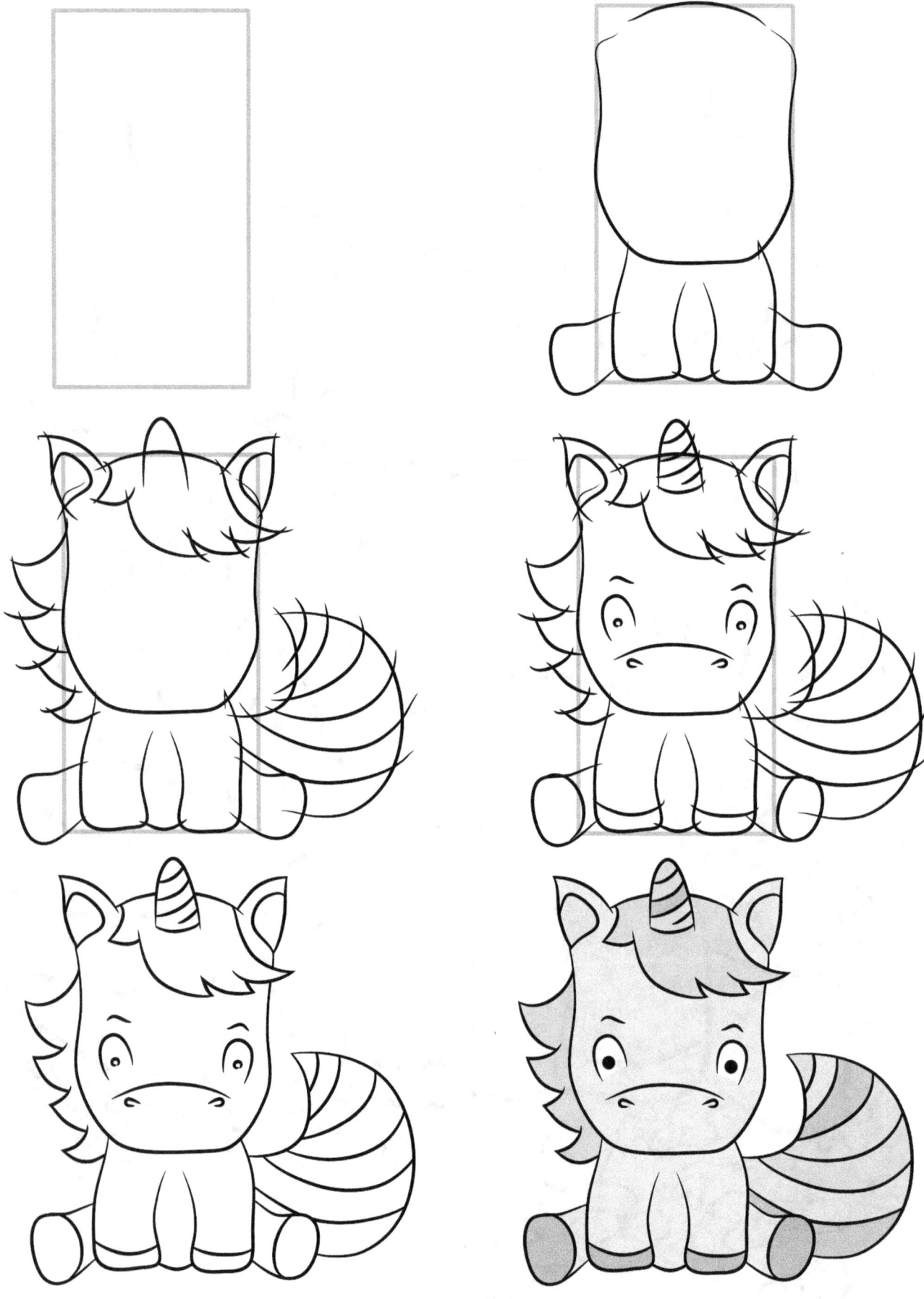

RABBIT

SIT

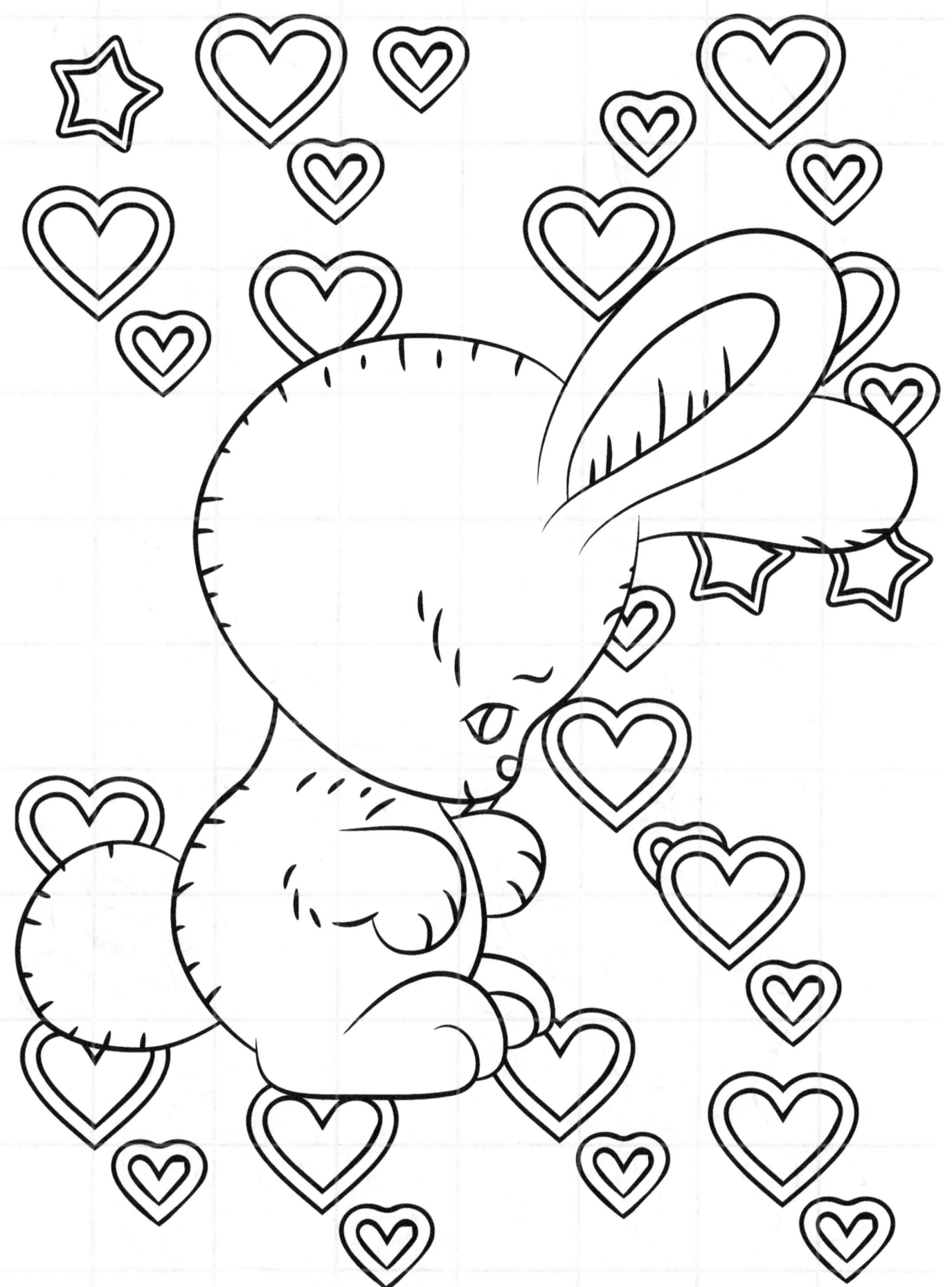

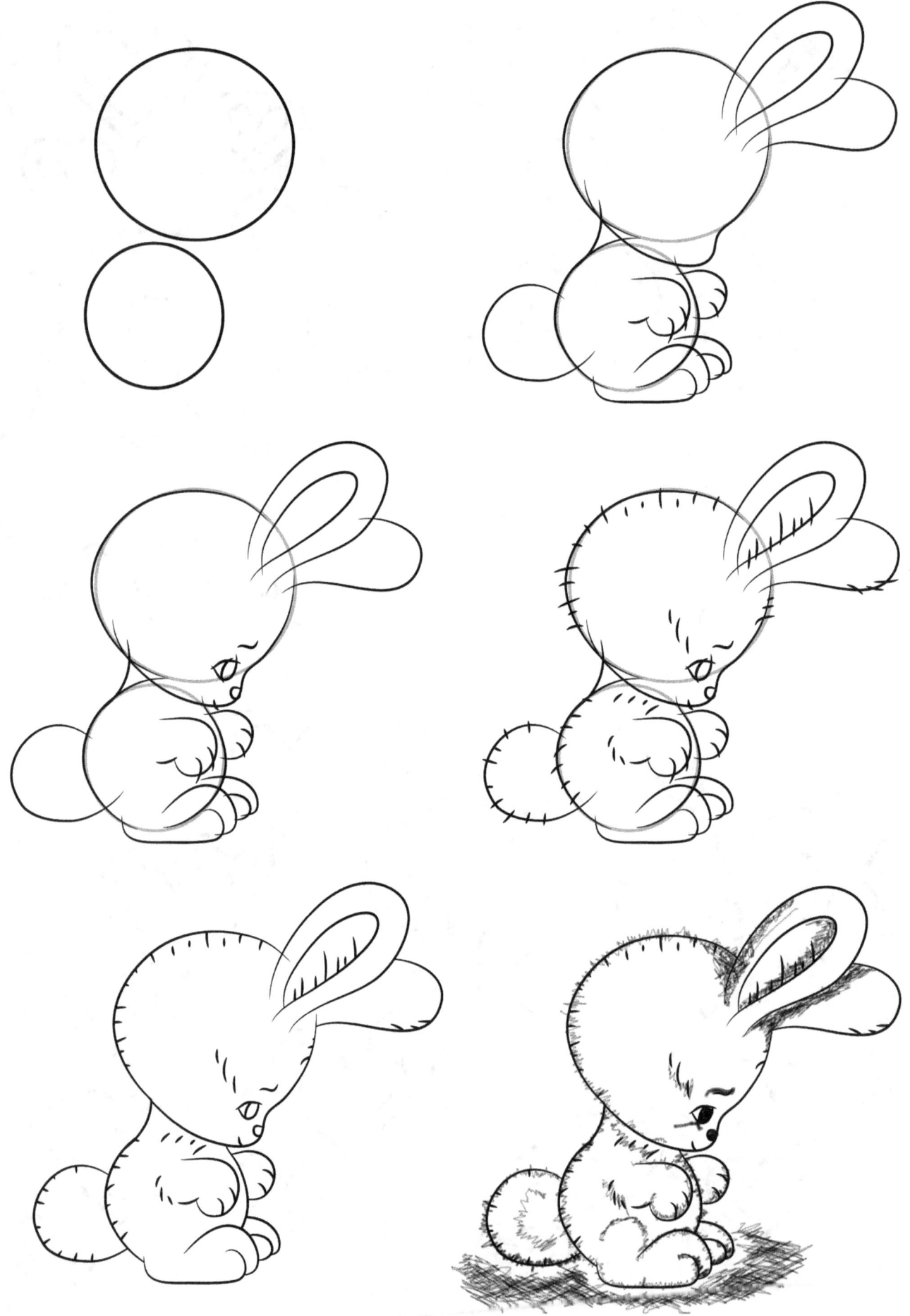

HOW TO DRAW CUTE ANIMALS FOR TODDLERS & KIDS

CUTE PETS FOR LEARN TO DRAW

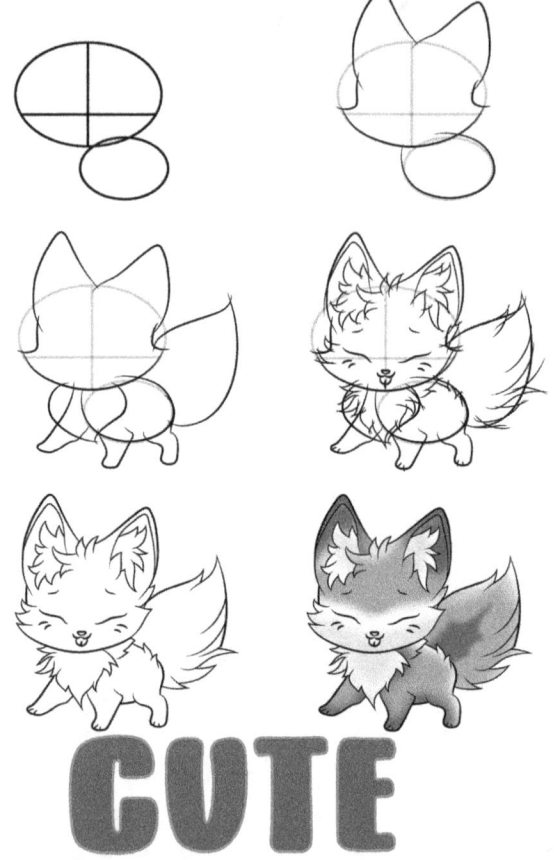

CUTE

FOR DRAWING

NEXT EDITION

COMONG SOON

www.ingramcontent.com/pod-product-compliance
Lightning Source LLC
Chambersburg PA
CBHW081007170526
45158CB00010B/2951